THE DAILY
SHIFT

—·—

IT'S NOT WHAT YOU THINK. IT'S BETTER THAN THAT

BECA LEWIS

PERCEPTION PUBLISHING

CONTENTS

DEDICATION

This book is dedicated to all the members of *The Shift Community* — especially to the extraordinary members of *The Women's Council*.

It is with love, patience, and consistency that they daily demonstrate the power of these Universal Spiritual Principles and Laws.

My thank you is larger than words can say.

— • —

ABOUT THE BOOK

Our lives are a projection of our thoughts and beliefs. These thoughts and beliefs build our perceptions, and it is our perceptions that determine what we experience.

The good news is that perceptions create nothing, they only hide from view what is already present; the abundance of the Infinite, which is so much better than what we think.

It is what I call the big R Reality.

We experience this Reality of Infinite Good more and more in our daily lives as we let go of limited thinking and perceptions, and shift to seeing Life as the I AM knows it to be.

To help you make that shift, I set this book up in *7–Day Shift Sessions.*

I wrote it so that the reader could read one day at a time, ponder its message, and then come back the next day for more on the same theme.

However, read the book the way that works best for you.

Read it all the way through, and then come back and just read a session a day, or pick a theme that you want to work on and start there.

It doesn't matter, it works best the way you want it to work!

If you would like to explore in more depth some of the concepts that mentioned throughout this book, you might like my other books in *The Shift Series*. You will find them listed at the end of this book.

My intent for this book is to provide a tool that can be returned to, repeatedly that will help bring all of your life's experiences into Infinite Good and meet your daily needs.

ONE

— • —

WEALTH

F or our first *7–Day Shift Session* we are going to immerse ourselves in the Truth about Wealth!

Understand that Wealth is something you already possess. Yes I know, it often doesn't feel that way, especially as the worldview is set up to encourage all of us to fear that there is not enough.

Most people succumb to this fear at one time or another, and become obsessed with finding ways to get more—usually money—because that is the currency we think is Wealth.

Have you ever noticed that when you are living in the fear of not enough and working hard to have enough, there is never enough?

We are going to start from the premise that the "not enough" is a lie. Why? Because, *What you perceive to be reality magnifies.*

If you and I agree with the worldview that there is not enough: There won't be—for you, for me, for anyone.

3

To release yourself and others to Wealth we all need to Wake Up! Wake up—Wake up—the W in Wealth.

To see and experience your Wealth and prosperity, the key is to decide to focus on the Wealth already present in your life. Not money. Wealth.

Money will follow when you decide to eliminate any thought about what you and others don't have.

Instead, focus entirely on what you do have.

Change your idea of Wealth to the qualities of Wealth evident in your life. Look for beauty, love, courage, grace, happiness, joy, etc.

Take time today to make a list of quality words that for you are Wealth, and then look for them in every person, place, or thing that crosses your path.

Enjoy the day fully awake and aware of the Wealth and prosperity that is evident when you decide to look for it.

Wealth is yours now!

WEALTH—DAY TWO

The E in Wealth stands for Enthusiasm. It is an essential ingredient to seeing and experiencing your Wealth and prosperity.

The original meaning of the word *Enthusiasm is divine inspiration, or a god within.*

If you used your quality list from yesterday at least a few times during the day, then probably you have already started to feel divine inspiration.

Today let's practice the invisible to feel and experience even more Enthusiasm.

The key to always seeing and experiencing your Wealth and prosperity is to have a variety of ways to corral your wandering thoughts that have drifted off to the worldview of lack, limitation, and fear, and bring them back to what you want to experience in your life.

Focus entirely on your qualities of Wealth.

Practice the invisible. Take your quality list—which will probably grow daily—and choose a quality or two from it to practice today.

For example: if you choose the quality of love as a quality of Wealth, today not only practice **seeing** it everywhere, but practice **being** it everywhere.

Ask yourself throughout the day, "Are my thoughts loving towards others? Are my thoughts loving towards myself?"

As you do this, expect to feel the divine inspiration of this practice.

In fact, practicing the invisible is the most fun you can experience once you get the hang of it and get in the habit. It can be done anywhere, anytime.

Enthusiasm is you! It's a brilliant day today.

WEALTH—DAY THREE

The A in Wealth stands for Angel Ideas, those marvelous ideas that seem to pop out of nowhere, bringing light to any situation.

These Angel Ideas are always immediately available. In fact, they are ready for you even before you ask for them. They wait for you to listen for them.

When you do, they bring you the solution to a problem, an idea for something new, a way to see something differently, and joy to the moment.

Angel Ideas are different than thoughts.

Thoughts keep us in the worldview by repeating back to us only what appears to be true, and then making it appear even more real by explaining why it must be true. Nothing about thoughts releases us from our current point of view.

Angel Ideas lift us above and out of the worldview.

For those people who don't honor Angel Ideas, they may appear to be the impossible, silly, never-been-done, how-will-that-work, can-I-really-do-that, kind of ideas. But, when we accept, honor, and love Angel Ideas, they are pure Wealth.

So today, listen and expect to hear and be moved by innumerable Angel Ideas, and revel in the delightful, brilliant light that they bring to every corner of your life, dissolving all limitations in the process.

Remember the phrase we all learned before crossing the street when we were kids: Stop, Look, and Listen. What a perfect reminder.

Before doing anything today, Stop, Look, and Listen for Angel Ideas. They are always there for you!

WEALTH—DAY FOUR

Love is the L in my interpretation of the word Wealth.

It seems obvious, doesn't it? If we have Love we are wealthy. However, we often do have Love and still don't feel wealthy or prosperous. There is something you can do to increase both Love and your experience of Wealth.

You can Love.

You can refuse to do anything but Love. No matter what the person, place or situation looks like, you can find something good to Love about it.

You can refuse to be tempted to discuss, think about, or be afraid of anything that does not appear to be good.

Why not try it for today?

You can think of it as a thought diet, instead of a food diet. Today you will avoid all those thoughts that are bad for you. Like magic, it will also affect anyone else within the radiance and radius of your thought.

Imagine that! Others will have the benefit of your diet.

Don't worry about how this thought diet will bring you Wealth and prosperity. In fact that worry is something that you are dieting from today. In this Love diet you can Love every second of the day. Don't hold back.

Stuff yourself with Love.

Feels good to be full of Love doesn't it?

The cool thing is, when you are filled up full with Love—well wait—I'll let you discover what happens!

Wealth—Day Five

Yes, you guessed it. Thanks is the T in my interpretation of the word Wealth.

What a privilege to be able to say Thanks. But how often do you do it? Very seldom! I know this to be true, because there are so many things for which all of us forget to be thankful.

7

I'll prove it.

Stop right now and look around you. Really look. No matter where you are, there are countless things that have been provided for you.

For example, you are reading this book! Think of that. Think of the millions of events that have taken place that have made it possible for you to be able to read this book wherever you are! Imagine what has been provided for you in each tiny part of the production of this book, the electricity, the software, etc.

Think of the dedication, energy, love, and care that so many people have given to create each element of what you so casually use.

You could spend hours giving Thanks just for the things you are aware of within the circle of your arms.

I know another thing that you are not thankful enough for: the talents that have been given to you.

No matter how good you are at giving Thanks for them, I know you have missed a few. Most of us have missed almost all of them. To rediscover your talents, start small.

Once again, start where you are sitting. What are you doing?

Think of the gifts and talents you have been given that allow you to do that. Expand out into your day, then your community.

Notice how you express unlimited talents and gifts each second of the day.

Give Thanks today. Give Thanks out loud when an Angel Idea moves you to speak. Give Thanks inside for everything.

Remember, we are seeing what has been given, and today we give Thanks.

Giving Thanks for you and your unique gifts and talents.

Wealth—Day Six

When I first heard the Angel Idea of using the word Wealth, I thought the H was Help Others. When I listened again, I realized that the Help means, "Help yourself first."

Before you can effectively help others, you must help yourself.

You are now. You are taking the time to redirect your thinking, to shift your perceptions, to know the truth about Wealth—because if you understand Wealth, you will have it and be able to share it.

But, what about other times? Have you ever found that you are distracting yourself from your true wishes and passion by helping others before you helped yourself?

Isn't this action one of the most draining, stifling and ultimately Wealth-stealing things you can do?

Yes it is; and in the end you have nothing left to help others with—no desires, no motivation, no resources. Sometimes we use this lack as a weapon against others. (Example: "I gave up all my dreams for you.")

Helping yourself first may take just a moment of thought-shifting, or many days, weeks, or months.

However, when you start with yourself, you will find that you will naturally move out into the world and ask, "How can I help you?"

You will be so filled with Wealth that sharing it, and using it, will become your nature. Your desire to help will expand into a dream bigger than yourself that will become the motive of your days and will outlive your personal time on earth.

So no matter how much you Help now, stop and **Help yourself first**, and then let that flow out of you into whatever action the Angel Ideas lead you to do.

WEALTH—DAY SEVEN

Together we have arrived at the 7th day of our shift to Wealth. This week you have learned how to use the word *Wealth* as your guide.

W—Wake Up, E—Enthusiasm, A—Angel Ideas, L—Love, T—Thanks, H—Help

During these last 7 days you have increased your understanding of True Wealth.

You have done this because you know that when you understand **this** Wealth, you will never worry about lack again.

Now that you have started this process, don't stop! Continue to practice the Truth about Wealth, just as you practice any other skill. Some days will feel easier than others, but the results will far outweigh any discomfort along the way.

What this practice will reveal to you is the treasure that can never be taken from you. It is one that you can spend with the assurance that it will never be depleted.

Never worry about the outcome of what you are guided to do. That is not your job.

You can't control what other people say, think, or do. Your job is to start with the correct premise in your own thinking and to constantly pay attention to your motives for all the actions you take, or don't take.

If you discover that you don't always walk in True Wealth, (none of us do yet) be thankful for that awareness, and then let it go.

Never hold on to those things you discover about yourself that are not beautiful and loving.

Don't say to yourself, "This is who I am" unless it is completely loving. Don't beat yourself up for your mistakes, big or small. Let them go.

Set yourself free to be and experience True Wealth.

I know that you are walking now in the light of the Truth about Wealth—and I am privileged to have been able to spend this time with you!

Wealth is you!

TWO

— ◦ —

LOVE

LOVE—DAY ONE

Let's talk about Love for the next *7–Day Shift Session*! It's the perfect choice because Love is a key component of understanding wealth.

We begin the same way as we did with wealth, understanding that it is something that you already possess. Once again, the worldview tries to make us believe there is not enough, and of course this distorted view applies to Love, too.

We are afraid that there is not enough Love to go around, or that we will do something that will cause us to be unlovable.

Since the worldview is in charge of manipulating what we see, until we take that control back, we will constantly be swamped with lies about Love.

People do despicable things under the guise of Love, but that is not Love at all, is it?

One of the most perfect descriptions of Love can be found in the Bible, I Corinthians 13, so let's use it as our premise of Love for these next 7 days.

Love is patient, love is kind.
It does not envy, it does not boast, it is not proud.
It is not rude,
It is not self-seeking,
It is not easily angered, it keeps no record of wrongs.
Love does not delight in evil but rejoices with the truth.
It always protects, always trusts, always hopes, always perse-
veres.
Love never fails.

This is the Truth about Love—imagine that!

Love—Day Two

Yesterday we discovered some of the qualities of Love. We learned that it is kind, patient, forgiving, protective, hopeful, trusting, good, and ongoing.

We also discovered what Love is not. It is not rude, self-seeking, easily angered, or revengeful.

The question for today is: Do you believe this to be True about Love? This is an important question to ponder. Don't just answer it off the top of your head. Think about it. Feel about it.

Throughout the day as you work, play, take care of home, family, and yourself ask yourself, "Do I believe that Love is kind, patient, forgiving, protective, hopeful, trusting, good, and ongoing—and that Love is not rude, self-seeking, easily angered, or revengeful?"

Pay attention to the answer. It may not be what you expect. Don't try to make up the answer; just listen.

Once you discover what you believe about Love it will so much easier to shift it to something even better. But if you lie to yourself and try to cover it up with positive thinking, nothing will ever permanently change for the better.

Don't get attached to what you discover. Just observe and keep notes.

LOVE—DAY THREE

What did you discover yesterday that you believe about Love?

Did it match our list? Do you believe that Love is kind, patient, forgiving, protective, hopeful, trusting, good, and ongoing—and not rude, self-seeking, easily angered, or revengeful?"

Whether you believed all of it, none of it, or some of it, there is one more step to take.

That is the step of asking yourself, **do you want this to be True**? Are you willing to give up any story that you have about Love that doesn't match these qualities?

This is a harder question to answer than what might appear on the surface. We all get something out of our "unloved and unlovable" stories.

But, is what we get worth holding onto these beliefs and stories? What if by giving them up we could experience perfect Love?

The question for today is one that carries with it great significance.

For today, ask yourself, "Am I willing to give up all the beliefs I have, and the stories I tell, that do not match the Truth about Love?"

You may find you are not willing to give these up yet, but that's okay.

If you tell the truth, it is the beginning of the end of their grip on you.

Once again, if you cover up these beliefs with positive thinking and don't completely face what is running your life, it will continue to be the unseen dictator that locks you away in a room by yourself, far from True Love.

Are you willing to Love and be Loved?

LOVE—DAY FOUR

At the beginning of this section on Love, we talked about the qualities of Love.

Yesterday I asked you if you were ready and willing to be loved and to Love, and to give up stories that keep this from happening.

So what if you did find a teeny tiny part of you that isn't willing to be loved or to Love, or even a big part of you that isn't willing to be loved or to Love because—get ready—there is good news here, because you have discovered one of those "monsters under the bed" that has been scaring you all these years.

Now that it has been seen, you can dissolve it with awareness and Truth.

Today will be fun because you are going to list all the reasons you are afraid of loving or being loved, otherwise known as "monsters under the bed."

Now, you may say that you have no resistance at all to Love, so if you really think that is true, skip this part.

But, if you are like the rest of us, there is a residual in there somewhere. Let me give you some possible ideas:

You might be secretly thinking, "Love is a responsibility. Do I want it?

Love means I have to give up part of myself. Love demands more than I have to give. Anybody that loves me must be crazy, so why would I Love them back?"

Do these prime the pump for you? So now you get to write down these kinds of thoughts. Don't worry, it won't create anything bad.

Your thoughts aren't creating anything they are only hiding what is. So writing them down will just bring them out in the open.

Have fun, no judgment, just observation.

LOVE—DAY FIVE

In this section we are practicing the qualities of Love found in the Bible, I Corinthians 13. We have agreed that Love is kind, patient, forgiving, protective, hopeful, trusting, good, and ongoing.

Did you have fun yesterday uncovering what we used to be afraid of, those "monsters under the bed"?

In reality these are only little "dust bunnies" of thoughts that have been clouding your Love view of these qualities in your life.

Let's sweep some of them away today with the broom of the Truth about Love.

Let me give you an example. Let's take the thought that you might have uncovered: that Love is a responsibility that is too much to handle.

Here's the thought:

"I can't handle the responsibility of Love."

Here's the broom:

"Since Love is gentle and Love is kind, the responsibility of Love must be to be gentle and kind. I find it easy to be gentle and kind to myself and others."

You can substitute any of the quality words you want to in your broom, or add them all. There are even more quality words you can add to your broom.

So if you think of them, write them down. In the meantime, start sweeping away those dust bunnies.

To make sure they don't return, you could pretend they are dust bunnies made of darkness and your broom is made of light. When the two meet, you know that the light will dissolve the darkness.

LOVE—DAY SIX

Yesterday we swept away the dust bunnies of thought that were clouding our ability to see the present availability of Love.

We used the broom of light with its strands of the qualities of Love to sweep those dark thoughts away, dissolving them into their native nothingness.

Now that our home, our consciousness, has been cleared out, we are prepared to be the qualities of Love ourselves.

It's easy to wish that others were more kind, patient, forgiving, protective, hopeful, trusting, good, and ongoing, but much harder to take responsibility to be those qualities ourselves.

But, it is here that we must begin and end, within ourselves.

Of course our desire is to be more kind, patient, forgiving, protective, hopeful, trusting, good, and ongoing to others; but really, we have to be all these qualities **to ourselves first.**

When we try it the other way around, sooner or later, something will throw us off balance and we will bounce back to what Love is not.

Or we may keep everything together on the surface, covering up a deep unhappiness.

When we begin by treating ourselves with Love first, we will have plenty of all the qualities of Love, like kindness, left over to spread to everyone we meet.

Happiness will begin within, blooming into an ongoing feeling that is consistently present, just like Love! So today is the day we pay attention to how we treat ourselves.

As yourself, "Am I being, kind, patient, forgiving, protective, hopeful, trusting, good, and ongoing to myself"? If yes, celebrate and do more. If not, well, you know the answer—since you are Love Loving Itself!

LOVE—DAY SEVEN

Hasn't this been a wonderful 7–Day Shift Session about Love?

We have rung the bell of Love this week, calling out to ourselves to see and be the qualities of Love.

We have stopped asking others to be something we are not practicing on ourselves. We have swept away the "monsters under the bed."

We have declared that Love Is Always Loving Itself, and that of course means us!

As we continue on this Daily Shift together, there are two things you can do.

First, you can celebrate with gratitude! You can fill up your heart with the gratitude that no matter it may seem in your life at this moment, Love is all there is. Love is filling all the spaces in your life.

Celebrate this as fact, knowing that nothing will ever change this Truth, and that you are awake and aware of the omnipresence of Love.

The second thing to do is to continue **to practice what you have started.**

Remember, the habit of a lifetime takes a discipline of habit to dissolve. Don't be discouraged by this. The dissolving of what is not true is a wonderful unfolding, just as a garden growing is a beautiful sight.

Let's end, as we began, with the description of Love found in the Bible, I Corinthians 13.

Love is patient, love is kind.

19

It does not envy, it does not boast, it is not proud.
It is not rude,
It is not self-seeking,
It is not easily angered, it keeps no record of wrongs.
Love does not delight in evil but rejoices with the truth.
It always protects, always trusts, always hopes, always perseveres.
Love never fails.

This is the Truth about Love—live it!

THREE

HOME

HOME—DAY ONE

In the first *7-Day Shift Session* we talked about wealth. In the second we focused on love. For the next 7-day session we are going to visit the concept of Home.

Everyone wants to feel wealthy, everyone wants to be loved, and everyone wants to have a Home. No matter how different our homes are, we all want a place where we feel we belong.

Home is not where you live, but where they understand you. —Christian Morgenstern

If we look at the concept of Home on the surface, it is just the place where we live. Some of us rent our homes; some of us own our homes. Some of us feel as if we have never had a "real" Home, and some of us are afraid of losing the Home we have.

Some of us are happy at Home; some of us feel trapped at Home.

There appears to be a wide gulf between those who have no Home to those who build huge and elaborate Homes, often to house just one or two people.

We have a multitude of TV programs and "make-money gurus" showing us how to build, decorate, flip, buy, sell, and make money from our homes.

There are huge industries built around the fear of not having a Home, or the greed of making money from our homes.

We need to ask this question: Is this what we mean by Home?

That is the focus of the next 7 days. What and where is Home?

When visiting sites on the web, we click the word Home as the place to return to.

We may also think of our personal Homes the same way. As T.S. Elliot said, *Home is where one starts from.*

Let's start there. To make this more personal, let's begin by exploring this question, "Where do you live?"

Richard Bach said, *The simplest questions are the most profound. Where were you born? Where is your home? Where are you going? What are you doing? Think about these once in a while and watch your answers change.*

Of course, you do remember that Home is not just a place, but also a *point of view,* and a *state of mind.*

HOME—DAY TWO

Yesterday we asked, "Where do you live?"—understanding that Home is not just a place, but also a point of view, and a state of mind.

What you want in a Home may not be what I want in a Home. Beginning with your own personal idea of the qualities of Home will ensure the process of living within the space, time, mindset, and actual structure that means Home to you.

Some qualities can change over time.

I have lived in the middle of a large city and in the middle of nowhere. Both homes brought me joy because for that time the qualities they offered exactly what I wanted. However, there are qualities that are important to me that have never changed, no matter where I lived.

What are those qualities of Home that have never changed for you? What kind of living experience are you looking for to call Home?

Are you looking for hustle and bustle, or silence? Do you want a view outside, or does the inside mean the most? Do you need outside space or inside space? Do you want privacy or lots of community interaction?

Choosing another person's idea of what Home means will never make us happy.

Imagine a turtle thinking what an elephant calls Home would work for him. Sounds ridiculous, but really that is what the worldview tries to sell us, that a Home is the same for everyone.

The Shift® always begins within, which means we start within ourselves to find the answers to what will then appear on the outside, including our homes.

It's true what Pliny the Elder said, *Home is where the heart is.*

Your heart: Where is it?

Home—Day Three

Love begins at home, and it is not how much we do, but how much love we put in that action.—Mother Teresa

Can a Home that begins with Love in action ever be devalued? Can this Home ever be taken from us? Of course not!

It also wouldn't matter if we actually owned a Home, or rented a Home, or lived in our car, if we began with, and stayed within, the Home of *Love in action.*

Beginning with Love in action, our homes are built on the solid rock of Truth. Then no matter how hard the wolf tries to blow it down, it will stand.

I had a friend who taught me the value of living the qualities of Home before, during, and after shopping for a Home.

She had a nice place to live, but her family was growing, and they wanted to move out of town to a quieter area and a bigger Home.

She began to study the qualities of what Home was to her and her family. She studied the promise of Divine Love: that the outcome of understanding and acting from Divine Love always provides for and meets every human need.

On the surface they didn't have enough money to buy the Home that was forming within her heart, but she never worried about it. She just kept learning more about the qualities of Home.

In the meantime she demonstrated Love in action in all that she did. For me, for two weeks she took my 3 very young children into her small Home where she already had 5 small children of her own, so I could attend a very important class.

This was typical of what she did. She didn't just speak Love, she acted Love.

Not long after that she easily moved her family into an even better home than they had originally desired. Those watching on the outside might have said it was "magic" that brought all the events that came into play to provide the Home.

But, it wasn't magic, it was a natural result of what my friend was doing. She knew where her heart was, and she demonstrated that knowing, through the living action of Love.

Isn't this a wonderful idea to practice, living the action of Love to discover Home!

HOME—DAY FOUR

I used to search for Home all the time.

Wherever I would go I would ask myself, "Could I live here, in this place, or in this Home?" I have asked myself that question in almost every state in the United States plus even in a few other countries.

What most confused me was that the answer was always "yes" and "no." Yes, I could see the beauty of each place and find joy in what it had to offer, and "no" because no place fulfilled something within me that was always searching for somewhere else.

Now I am learning that the human idea of myself will always search, but it always searches within the idea of human; and the answer will never be found there. The human point of view is the lack of understanding of Oneness, so no matter how long we search within that point of view for anything, we will never find it.

I realized that I could have a house in every location I have ever loved, and still I would not feel at Home—until I understood completely that Home is not a physical place or dwelling, it is a spiritual fact.

Home is where the heart is, but not the human heart. Home is in the heart of Love.

It doesn't matter whether we are in a car, the woods, a hotel, a train, a resort, a castle, or a store. It doesn't matter if the view is ocean, woods, field, rocks, desert, or the city; if we remain present in the awareness of Where I Am is Home, then Home is where we are.

Beginning with the correct premise of Home, then it doesn't matter what the worldview says about where we live.

As we stay within our own awareness of the qualities that make up the idea of the Home, this awareness automatically translates to what appears as a physical Home, which matches more and more those qualities that we already live within, in the Heart of Love.

If that doesn't appear true to you, look again; but look through the lens of the qualities of Home, not the physical measurements of size, cost, and location.

Everything has already been provided, including Home. We must just learn to look differently to see it.

HOME—DAY FIVE

My home has always been show business.—Sammy Davis, Jr.

This is another way to look at Home. Home as the way we express ourselves.

Have you ever experienced doing something so completely that everything vanished except you and what you were doing?

Did it matter where you were at the time? Did you feel content, safe, secure, inspired, happy and content?

Aren't these all qualities that we want to feel when we are Home?

As a writer, a place that I feel most at Home is when I am writing. Sometimes I write better in cafes, other times I love the stillness of someplace I have never been before. Most of the time it is at my desk, but it isn't the place that gives me peace, it is the doing.

Home is where we are thinking and doing what we love; Home is much more than where our physical body lives.

Of course, as we become aware of the qualities of Home, honor them, rejoice in them, and realize that they are ever-present in every area of our lives, this internal shift will express itself into a better and better picture of Home that matches our own idea of the qualities of Home, not another's idea of Home.

This is an important key. Home does not look the same to everyone, just as the way we spend our day and express ourselves is not the same. We do not need, require, or want the same type of Home as another.

There is no value in feeling less than another because our Home is not as grand as theirs. In fact the feeling of "less than" begins within.

It begins with thinking that we are not as important or grand as another; and it is within our thinking that we must dissolve it.

We are each unique expressions of the One Mind. Comparing ourselves to another is ludicrous since there is no "other." There is only One Mind expressing itself.

Wanting what we don't have, wanting what others have, throws us out the door of our ever permanent Home within the One Mind, into the wilderness of human thinking.

Once we stop that comparison, we can pick ourselves back up and enter again into the true idea of Home.

Ask yourself, "When do I feel the most at Home?" Listen quietly and patiently for the answer, and it will reveal itself to you.

HOME—DAY SIX

Welcome to the silence, Feel your heart's alliance, Close your eyes, Breathe in the empty space, Welcome home to the sweet state of grace.—Johnny Elkins, from the musical Leap.

The dictionary defines grace as the unmerited divine assistance given to humans. Reading this definition, most of us feel a sense of disquiet. This is not what we know grace to be. It is much more than that.

The problem with this definition is that it is within the worldview and about the worldview.

It implies that grace pops into our lives periodically without warning and gives us some assistance even though we didn't do anything to deserve it. It breaks human laws and gives us some respite from the limitation and lack within the worldview.

But this isn't Divine Grace, is it? Grace is a living state of being; it is the spiritual presence of Divine Love, felt, lived, enjoyed, and acknowledged. Not because we are humans and deserve it, but because we are the action of the spiritual presence of Grace.

The best way to find our Home in grace is to live it. Grace is not a dead idea. We can't just sit on the couch and say "grace will take care of it." We have to live the qualities and ideas of grace to actually feel its presence.

As we see, acknowledge and then live the beauty of grace, the joy of grace, the safety of grace, and the love of grace, we find ourselves at Home in the state of living in grace.

At peace in this awareness, and trusting in its truth, we can rest in the knowledge that wherever we are, grace is always present.

Grace does not break human laws—it supersedes them. It overrides the worldview illusion and brings us into the safety of the spiritual law of Divine Love.

Daily we can say to ourselves, "Welcome Home, dear one, to the sweet state of grace, the perfect and only real Home."

Home—Day Seven

Pilgrim on earth, home and heaven are within thee. —Walford Davies

We have traveled far these last few days in our search for Home. We have moved from thinking Home is a building to understanding that Home is a point of view and a state of mind.

We have dismissed the belief that Home is something we own, or must acquire.

We have sighed in relief over the awareness that grace is where we live, not something we have to earn, but only to acknowledge and understand.

Since *what we perceive to be reality magnifies* we can trust that as we continue this awareness, while dropping our baggage containing our preconceived notions, fears, regrets, and sorrows, we will no longer live with clipped wings within a human concept of Home.

Instead, we continue to discover that we are free to live wherever we are, whatever Home may look like.

We celebrate that we are always living within the many mansions of Divine Love.

Someday we will all learn to speak and live from the Truth at all times, but in the meantime, we can begin by acknowledging it within our hearts.

Because we know this is not a material world, we can fully acknowledge the Truth in this promise, and trust its provision: *In my Father's house are many mansions: If it were not so, I would have told you. I go to prepare a place for you.*—John 14:2

Our Home has been prepared long in advance of our needing it. Let's let grace carry us over its threshold to live there as intended, "happily ever after."

FOUR

— ◆ —

PURPOSE

PURPOSE—DAY ONE

The next *7–Day Shift Session* will be very exciting because we are going to talk about Purpose. Once again I am going to use the letters in a word—this time the word Purpose—as our starting point.

For such a glorious subject, the idea of living from Purpose can feel like a burden rather than a blessing when we think we don't understand our own Personal Purpose.

Personal—that is the P in Purpose.

Personal, meaning your unique expression of Infinite Mind; not personal, as in personality. This is an important distinction.

If our Purpose is defined in terms of personality, then it would revolve around a limited human sense, with both positive and negative aspects. That would imply that those with charm and presence would seem to have a higher Purpose than those who have different ways of expressing themselves.

In society, we make the mistake of following personality instead of substance. In fact we are taught that if we follow the personality of others, we may actually be able to look like them, or be like them, too.

The Personal that I am referring to is becoming aware of yourself as the unique idea and action of Infinite Mind. To make this easier to talk about, I call this your USB, or Unique Spiritual Blessing. This is something that radiates as you, without effort.

It will produce the same response as looking at a flower and feeling what it has to offer without any effort on its part. Each flower's Purpose is Personal to it. It couldn't stop doing what it is even if it tried.

This is the same for you.

No matter how hidden from view it may be, you have a Personal Purpose —Unique Spiritual Blessing—that you radiate without effort. To discover your USB can often take time to uncover until it becomes the cornerstone, or Purpose, of our lives, but it can and must be done. Tomorrow we'll talk about ways to begin to uncover your Personal USB.

Purpose—Day Two

Today we are going to Uncover—the U in Purpose—your Unique Spiritual Blessing.

Your USB is something that you can't stop yourself from doing, no matter how hard you may try. However, for most of us this is an elusive idea.

In fact, when I first teach this concept, almost everyone first comes up with something negative about themselves.

It's a start, but not the end. Your USB is a positive, like the perfume from a rose, that affects everyone equally who is willing to "stop and smell" it.

Our USB is often the easiest thing in the world for us to do, so we are inclined to think it is useless, or not very important. It is often the thing we did as a child that we were told to stop. Usually this is because we didn't know how to present it with finesse.

The negative that you may first think is your Purpose does contain clues that will guide you to your real USB, but the negative is never your Purpose or who you are.

I'll use myself as an example. Examining my life, I realized that I couldn't stop myself from shifting people's perception.

As a child I would often say (to adults too), "If you look at this differently then you could do what you want to do; or you wouldn't be stuck; or things would be better."

Since this rarely produced a good result for me, I came to view this behavior as a negative, and told myself to shut up. But no matter how hard I tried to make myself stop talking about shifting perceptions, I did it all the time anyway.

As a choreographer I would say to a dancer who couldn't do a step, "Show me how you can't do it." The result was a shifted perception on the other dancer's part, and an ability to do what she thought she couldn't do.

You can see that as an adult I had begun to temper how I shifted perceptions, and it is still a skill I am learning.

But, I couldn't, and still can't, stop myself from doing this no matter what profession or job I am doing.

As a child I wasn't graceful or discerning about my purpose, so I tried to stop it. Actually, everyone tried to stop me from doing it, because I was very annoying.

I can still be annoying, but at least I now know and accept my USB, and I practice being more graceful and mindful in its execution.

Look back at your own life; do you see your USB hiding within the folds of your life?

Tomorrow we will discuss the revealing of your Purpose to yourself.

Purpose—Day Three

The word Reveal is our R in Purpose. It is not the words resist, replace, or even renewal. It is Reveal.

Why? Because your unique Purpose is not something that has to be renewed, nor replaced with something else, nor resisted. It only needs to be Revealed.

As you looked back through your life, did you find a common thread?

If you look at your daily activities, do they all stem from one common desire? Are there things that you do that bring you more joy than others? What part of them?

One place to get these answers is to ask people who know you. Just as it is often easier to see another's faults than it is to see our own, it is often easier to see the basic essence of another than it is to see our own.

Why go to the trouble of Revealing your Purpose?

Imagine living each moment in the now, enjoying what you are doing, finding reason for your being that can never be taken away.

And, it is even more than that.

Each of us is an integral idea in Infinite Mind.

This means that it takes all of us expressing our Unique Spiritual Blessing to be the full completeness of the I AM.

No matter how hard we may try to hide from the Truth about ourselves, it is always present.

The word "hard" gives us a clue; because it is much harder to hide from the Truth than it is to release ourselves to living as a unique action of Truth.

Let your uniqueness be Revealed to you, and release yourself to the relief and joy that this awareness will reveal.

PURPOSE—DAY FOUR

Does your Purpose Provide? Is it your Provision? Yes it does, and yes it is. These two words are our next P in the word Purpose.

Provide and Provision.

Let's start by looking at the definitions of these two words that are linked together in meaning.

Provide: "To make preparation to meet a need."

Provision: "A measure taken beforehand to deal with a need."

Wouldn't it be wonderful if we understood both through our heartfelt awareness and our logical thinking sense—that our Unique Spiritual Blessing is our Provision?

Wouldn't it be a relief to fully realize that our Purpose is our Provision, the pre-planned, prepared, taken beforehand measure, that Provides for us?

The Truth is, who we are is Mind knowing itself.

If we fully understood this, wouldn't we be more willing to undercover and live our Purpose, instead of busying ourselves with things to do, so we could buy more things, own more things, and control more things?

Wouldn't we be more willing to step out of the Dilbert Cube of the worldview and live as our USB? Take a moment and think it through. Would Divine Love that is Infinite Intelligence always take care of Itself? Of course!

Therefore, since we are the Ideas and Action of Divine Love, Loving Itself,it makes perfect sense that who we are is Provision Itself.

Of course, it doesn't make sense, if we are determined to hold on to our own personal personality ego, and the point of view that we are the ones in control and that we are personal creators.

Since this personal sense does not really Provide, nor contain our true Purpose, at some point we all must become willing to give it up.

When we give up personal sense, we arrive at the Provision of Purpose. This makes the exploration of the Revealing of Purpose a task worth doing.

PURPOSE—DAY FIVE

When I was writing this, I had a bird feeder that hung just outside of my second-floor window. At different times of the day and different times of the year I had a multitude of different kinds of birds that visited the feeder.

After watching them for two years, something become very obvious to me.

I could see that each bird is entirely Original, even within the same species.

Original is our O in Purpose.

Each of us is an Original and unique action and idea of the Divine Intelligence called God. It takes concentrated observation to be able to tell the birds at the feeder apart, the same way it takes dedicated observation to see your Original expression of your Purpose.

To be accurate, all of us have just one Purpose: to be what we are, which is God in action.

However, the infinity and originality of what appears to us as the universe makes it clear to us that every idea of God has an Original way that Purpose is fulfilled.

Uncovering and revealing your USB, your Unique Spiritual Blessing, is the Purpose of these 7 days.

Depending on your state of mind and point of view, this is either an exciting treasure hunt, with the pot of gold being the discovery of your own Original expression, or it's an exercise in futility.

Think of it: we are each the Original idea of Infinite Intelligence. What an amazing Love this Divine Mind must have for each of Its Original Ideas —one of which appears as you.

Let's choose the point of view that reveals the treasure chest of joy that is the inevitable outcome of living your Purpose as an Original idea of Divine Mind!

Purpose—Day Six

Let's look at one more definition, the definition of Purpose, which is: "Something to set up as an object or end to be attained."

It is interesting that the word Purpose comes from the word meaning "intend" or "by intent; intentionally."

Now let's look at that definition of Spiritually, our S in the word Purpose, and see how it applies to each of us.

By Spiritually I mean "seen without the material overlay, or the human personality ego, or the worldview training."

As best as we can imagine, let's look at it as God would. Would you do a little mental adventure exercise with me? Here we go!

Since we know that what we call human is really the compound idea of God, then couldn't we say that we are God's Purpose?

Let me give you an example, using the sun as a symbol. The result of the sun, being itself, is light.

The beams of light that appear to come from the sun is a misperception. We see the light broken up into beams because of the dust, or impurities, in the air.

If the dust particles or impurities in the air weren't present, then we would see the light from the sun as it is, unbroken, undivided, and everywhere.

The sun is seen because of its action, or expression, or idea, we call light. That is the sun's intent and Purpose: light.

God, by being All, is "seen" because of Its action, or expression, or ideas we call individual humans, only because we are looking through an imperfect lens of perception.

A clear awareness, without the imperfection of our mist-perception, would reveal only the I AM or the Us that is the I AM. That would mean we are God's Purpose, or God's Intent.

Think on that, my friends. If nothing else, it will expand your awareness of the infinity of the Purpose of God that we call "me" and what we call our own personal Purpose.

Purpose—Day Seven

Now that we have reached the seventh day in our exploration of looking at Purpose differently, I hope that I have given you an idea of the Expansion of Purpose. Yes, the E in Purpose is Expansion.

When we think of our Purpose as a badge of personal honor or obligation, we are within the human realm of personality and ego, and not in the freedom of knowing that Purpose is the outcome of Love Knowing Itself.

Too often, we get stuck in doing something, or being something, because we think it is linked to a "calling" we have to answer. The Expansion of our Purpose may appear as something to do, but this is not where we start.

We start with Truth and listening within, to the sweet Original song that is you. As you listen within you will know what action to take that will lead you to a Purpose-filled life by singing your clearest song.

It will be the one that you knew all along.

Your clearest song, your Purpose, is the one that you have been observing these last 7 days, and you have been translating it back to its spiritual origin.

As you continue Uncovering and Revealing, the Expansion of your Purpose is the natural outcome.

The only obligation that you have is to come away from the human prison of personal Purpose, and into the freedom of Divine Mind's Purpose, seen as you.

Five

Happiness

Happiness—Day One

A braham Lincoln said, *Most folks are as happy as they make up their minds to be.* This is a perception-shifting statement isn't it? Of course this is true, but the problem is, how do we make up our minds to be happy?

The United States' Constitution says we have the right to pursue Happiness. It doesn't actually say we have the right to be happy.

So why not go to a higher power than the Constitution, and claim our right to be happy?

It's the words "right to be" that are the key to the puzzle of how to make up our minds to be happy.

If we have been trained to feel as if we don't have a right to happy, then being happy may feel wrong.

For the next 7 days, let's shift that "taught to us perception" of not having a right to be happy, to knowing absolutely that not only do we have a right to Happiness, but that Happiness is a quality that is innate in each one of us, and we can and will find it and live it.

There are many causes and reasons for unhappiness, but in the end there is only one way to be happy.

This is the good news, isn't it; because when we learn how to choose and accept Happiness, we will eliminate all those reasons and causes of unhappiness.

There's no time like the present to be happy, so let's get started!

Each day for the next 7 days I will give you a short and simple exercise to eliminate unhappiness and reveal Happiness.

Here's your exercise for the day. It's just one question.

Who do you think is happier than you?

HAPPINESS—DAY TWO

Today is an observation day. As we have talked about in the past shift series, in order to shift our perceptions, and not just cover them up, we need to know our current point of view.

We have to discover the hidden beliefs and perceptions, and even the not-so-hidden beliefs and perceptions, in order—in this case—to be utterly happy for apparently no good reason.

Think of this as your big cleaning out the closet day.

You know, the day you take all your clothes out and decide which ones you want to keep, and which ones don't fit or don't make you look good. It may produce a messy room for a bit, but in the end, it feels great.

Ready? Your exercise today is a series of questions.

Here we go:

- Did you make a list of who you think is happier than you?

- Was it hard or easy to do?

- Is it okay with you that some people are happier than you?

- Would you rather that I had asked who is sadder than you?

- What do those people, who are happier than you, have —that you don't have—that allows them to be so happy?

- If you had the exact thing they do, would you allow yourself to be happy?

- If you were really happy all the time, what would your best friend, spouse, parents, and children say?

HAPPINESS—DAY THREE

When I was a teenager I alternated between Happiness and depression. When I was depressed, I wrote poems about depression and left them around where I was sure my mom would see them, since I believed that a large portion of my unhappiness was my parents' fault.

Perhaps all teenagers think it's their parents' fault that they are unhappy; but we are adults now and able to take full responsibility for our own Happiness.

To shift our past perception that is affecting our current Happiness, we can "revisit" scenes from the past, and see them through different eyes.

Instead of the person we were then, we can be the awareness that we are now.

Don't worry about which scene from the past is the most important; just take the one that occurs to you now and re-see it.

Visit it now as an aware adult who understands that Divine Love has always been present.

See it with the Truth that you have never been abandoned or betrayed or damaged.

Yes, I know that the memory is often these very things. However, if we want to be happy, we need to rewrite the script. **It is not changing Truth; it is re-seeing what happened as a lie about the Truth.**

You'll get better at this as you let go of the idea that what happened was real, and therefore must be suffered for or paid for. It's not, and it doesn't.

What can you lose? Try out a scene and see what happens.

Move on to the next one. Would you rather be right about the past, or happy in the present? You choose.

Here are your two questions for the day.

- Whose fault is it when you are unhappy?

44

- Why?

In order to be utterly happy the only thing necessary is to refrain from comparing this moment with other moments in the past, which I often did not fully enjoy because I was comparing them with other moments of the future.—Andre Gide

HAPPINESS—DAY FOUR

Yesterday we asked, "Whose fault is it that you are unhappy, and why?" Of course, we often feel as if someone or something else has done something that has caused us to be unhappy.

We can be unhappy due to jobs, income, parents, spouses, children, living conditions, health issues, too much or too little money, governments, terrorists, mosquitoes, too hot or too cold—okay, you and I know that I could go on with this list forever.

Nevertheless, doesn't everyone face all these issues at one time or another, and yet some people are always happy anyway?

So if we have to assign fault to anyone, it really must come back to us.

This is actually good news, because it makes it easier to be happy, since we don't have to fix anyone or anything else.

All we have to do is shift our own perception to an awareness and acceptance of Happiness.

However, we can sometimes feel so unhappy, we can't remember what makes us happy.

Happiness list of why and what makes us
...ndy. I made a list like this once. I was sitting
...lized that I was happy for the first time in

I g... piece of paper and a pen and started writing
down what made me happy, so if I forgot I could get out the
list and remember.

There were simple things on that list, starting with sitting in
a good café, and then I added reading a good book, going to
the movies, getting a child to smile at me, etc.

None of what was on the list was "profound," they were all
simple activities. I kept that list, and every time I found myself
feeling unhappy I did something on the list. It always worked.

As I expanded my awareness of the quality of Happiness, I
rarely needed to look at the list anymore, but it was a great place
to start.

This your assignment for the day.

- See yourself as happy.

- What are you doing?

- What are you thinking?

- Start a list!

*The smallest fact is a window through which the infinite may
be seen.*—Aldous Huxley

HAPPINESS—DAY FIVE

Sometimes we are happy, but we act unhappy and don't realize it.

I had a vivacious grandmother who was a lover of life. However, she constantly complained under her breath. I am sure she had no idea at all that she was doing it.

I have a clear memory of her looking under the sink trying to get something out and the running commentary of her complaining while she was doing it. I do that same thing sometimes. When I am observing myself, I am amazed that it is happening.

Family habit! It can be dissolved!

She was happy, I am happy. However, if you heard that complaining, would you know?

When we complain, either consciously or unconsciously, we are reinforcing the human computer program that produces what we perceive as our life.

This program doesn't know that we are happy; it doesn't know we don't mean what we are complaining about.

It "hears" unhappiness and assumes that is what we want more and so it shrinks our perception down to what it thinks we believe, actually reducing the possibilities of our lives.

Or, said more simply, *What we perceive to be reality magnifies.*

It's up to us to choose a different reality.

If you are reading this, you either want to, or have already chosen, the point of view of the Reality of Infinite Mind. The next step, which is imperative, is to actually live in Reality, to consciously choose the state of mind that reinforces this point of view.

Consciously choose Happiness, consciously stay in the state of mind of Happiness, and it will reveal what is already true: that Happiness is, because divine Love is. To help us get to, and stay in, this state of mind, our new habit will be to observe Happiness. What does it look like?

So here is your question for the day.

- Who is the happiest person you know?

Happiness is not a matter of intensity, but of balance, order, rhythm, and harmony.—Thomas Merton

HAPPINESS—DAY SIX

It's spring as I write this. Although I grew up in Pennsylvania, I lived in California as an adult.

Every spring I would say to my family in the East, "Yes it is spring here too," and they would smile and say, "Hum."

And now that I am back in the East I know what they meant. The spring here is even more intense.

We wait for spring with a passion.

In February I look in vain for signs of spring. A little green shoot—anything.

When spring does come, it sweeps in like the wind. One day it is dark and dreary, and the next the trees are wearing gorgeous halos of red and yellow buds.

The daffodils are not visible one day, and nodding their golden heads in the breeze the next. You have to carefully watch each day not to miss spring as it bursts forth from winter.

The harbingers and celebrators of spring are the birds. They sing with every fiber of their being. I watched a tiny goldfinch belt out a song that could be heard around the block. Sitting on the tree limb it glowed with Happiness.

Yes, this is all about Happiness.

Buried beneath what may appear as a winter of unhappiness are the seeds of Happiness—just waiting for the warmth of love to burst forth.

I can see each of you on your tree of life, singing of joy with every fiber of your being.

Before the sun comes up, the bird begin their dawn chorus of song. You can begin now too, knowing that nothing can stop the sun, or your Happiness from rising.

Your assignment today:

- Wherever you live, get up early enough to listen to the morning chorus of birds. Imagine how it must feel to be filled with as much joy and love of life.

HAPPINESS—DAY SEVEN

We began this *7–Day Shift Session* with the realization that we have a right to be happy, and an awareness of why we might have unconsciously chosen to not be happy.

We followed up with some tools we can use to let go of those reasons, and to live as Happiness itself.

There is no reason to stop at a sort of happy place.

As we understand the true nature of Love as the only presence, the only activity, the only cause and creator, then the mist of false perceptions of what claim to be situations and circumstances that produce unhappiness will dissolve.

This allows us to see Happiness as a basic element and quality of life.

With this understanding of Happiness, all the reasons for unhappiness are eliminated in one fell swoop, because they all begin and end from the false premise of duality and separation.

Now that you have cleaned out your mental closet, don't go putting those old beliefs and perceptions back in.

Be careful about what you choose to perceive.

- Don't buy all that stuff that claims that suffering is necessary and that we must be unhappy to be good.

- Check your closet often to make sure unhappiness has not slipped back in without your noticing.

- Daily give yourself full permission to be utterly and unreasonably happy.

- Pull out your list of what makes you happy once in awhile and do something on it. Sing with the birds at least once a season, and experience what they know.

- Continue with this Happiness shift so that when

you ask the question, "Who is the happiest person I know?" you will be able to answer without hesitation, "It is me!"

Celebrating Happiness!

Six

—◦—

Intent

Intent—Day One

Is there something you want?

Of course there is!

We are all filled with wants and desires, and depending on what point of view we are in when we want something, and what point of view we are in when we take action to receive what we want, we are either frustrated or fulfilled.

It's interesting how on the outside the same action can convey many different points of view. An aware observer can tell the difference through the fruits of those actions and the methods employed.

If we are in the worldview—the dualistic, lack, fight-to-survive point of view—it will easy be to witness the fearful, competition-to-win, me-first methods, which people employ to get what they want.

When we are in the One Mind, only one cause and creator, and we are living Divine Love Loving Itself, well—it's easy to see that we will be much more likely to operate with kindness, joy, courage, and sharing.

A wonderful example of this happened with a high school girl's softball team.

The girl at bat hit her first home run ever, but as she reached first base her knee gave out. Her own team was not allowed to help her, so the opposing team carried her around the bases knowing full well that the run she hit was the winning run.

What do you think that team's Intent was?

It's easy to see that they were coming from Love Loving Itself. The results of this action will carry the fruits of their action far past that one game, into inspiring others to think differently.

This was different from setting a goal to win, isn't it? It is clear in this action that Intent and goals need to be placed in the proper order.

We are taught goals first, Intent last—if ever.

For the next 7 days, let's put Intent first, and let goals be the outcome, not the cause. To do this, we need to understand the difference, which will be one of the results of these 7 days.

- In the meantime, why not make a list of things you want?

It's not bad to want something, so go for it. By the end of the week you will be much clearer about what that list means.

INTENT DAY TWO

Whoever has the clearest Intent wins.

Oh gosh I know, this doesn't sound very spiritual given that someone "wins," but it is true.

Let me give you a few scenarios to clarify what I mean.

You go to the grocery store with the Intent of buying just a few items. On the way through the aisles you pick up many more items, and maybe even a few more as you check out.

Who had the clearer Intent, you or the grocery store?

You have a perfectly clear Intent not to eat dessert at the family gathering. However, once there, everyone teases you about it and you feel guilty for not eating, so you join them. Who has the clearer Intent. You or the rest of the family?

You decide to spend the day doing something you really want to do, but a friend calls and asks you to go with her to do an errand. Who has the clearest Intent: you or your friend?

You see, I am not saying one is right and one is wrong; it's just that when we are not clear about our Intent, or the reasons for our Intent, we are very often swayed to another person's plans.

However, it is actually very easy to end up with two clear Intents and both parties being happy with the outcome.

As I began the writing of this day, my husband asked me if I wanted to go to the movies with him and a few other members of our family.

Yes, I did want to go to the movies, and I was tempted to drop everything and go.

However, I had a very clear Intent, and reasons for my Intent, so I was happy to say "no" and neither of us felt badly about my decision to stay at work, or about his decision to go to the movies.

For your assignment today, choose one thing off of your list of what you want, which you made yesterday, and listen within for the reasons you want it.

Add those reasons to your list.

Enjoy yourself. This is a fun week!

Intent—Day Three

Did you come up with reasons for why you want something on your list?

Whether it was hard or easy, do you see how these reasons are the foundation for Intent? Once you know them, it will be much easier to keep your Intent—which really means keeping your word to yourself.

To illustrate the next step in our clarifying Intent process, let me give you some of the reasons behind my Intent to get my work done yesterday and not to go to the movies.

My reasoning went something like this: "I have a commitment to others to have this piece of writing done. If I finish my writing and my business obligations, I will be able to take a week off to see my daughter and grandchildren without taking my work with me.

"Also, since we are moving in a few weeks, I know that I will want to spend time designing our new home environment. If I don't complete these tasks before I leave I will not have the freedom to do this."

Notice that I had clear reasons, and that they were also attached to a feeling.

I compared the brief feeling of taking time off to go to the movies, and the deeper longer-lasting feeling of having freedom to visit with loved ones and to design some spaces, something I find joy in doing. After doing that, it was easy to know what my Intent was, I honored it, and so did my husband.

I once stopped eating something that I didn't want to be eating, because I compared how I felt when I didn't eat it, to how I felt when I did.

Reasons attached to feelings will help you clarify any Intent.

Notice I did not say emotions. Emotions are based in the dualistic human worldview; when we act from emotion, we will most often get the exact opposite of our true Intent.

- Let's go back to your list. You picked something you want, and you gave reasons for why you want it.

- Now take some quiet time, and feel why you want it. What feelings does it give you?

You may discover in this process that you don't want it at all, or you may also find that you already have it, hidden in plain sight.

INTENT—DAY FOUR

Most of us equate being busy with living fully. However, if we are not clear about our own Intents, being busy is just a way to run and hide from our true desires.

This makes it even more important to to get clear about Intent.

Clear Intents are the way to become much less busy, happier, calmer, and more abundant than ever.

Now that we've added reasons and feelings to our list of what we want, let's talk about the difference between Intents and goals, so that we don't get confused by the two.

They are entirely different.

We live in a goal-orientated world. We are encouraged to write our goals down each year, otherwise known as New Year's resolutions.

Then later we get to face up to what we did or didn't do with our goals or resolutions.

Even when we actually do accomplish our goals, it rarely produces a feeling of satisfaction, unless we started the goal process with Intent first.

Goals fade away, or we forget that we made them, while our Intent remains long afterwords, because we have reasons and feelings about it.

Goals can only be stated from what we already know about, while Intent begins with "imagine what if."

Goals begin from the outside and are imposed on our thinking and feelings, which often rebel.

Intent begins internally, which is actually where all that appears to be external begins.

Goals can breed fear of failure and fear of success, while Intent reveals what has already been perfectly created—so there is no place for fear.

Goals require continual effort and out-putting of energy.

Intent allows effortless action.

- Let's go back to your list. Now that you have a clear

Intent about at least one item on your list, let's do one more thing.

- No, not make a goal list; make a what do I think I have to do to get this list.

- Write everything down. All of it, even the parts you don't like. I'll tell you what to do with them tomorrow.

Intent—Day Five

The word *Intent* carries with it an unspoken agreement, and that agreement is that you are willing to do what it takes; any of it and all of it.

Sometimes we wonder why nothing happens after we have stated our Intent.

Often it is because we have an unconscious—and sometimes not-so-unconscious—aversion to doing a part of what it would take to accomplish or even allow the Intent to take place.

Somewhere hidden within our choices, we have that feeling, "that would mean I might have to," and whatever that "might have to" is, we feel we could not handle it, or we are not willing to do what would be required.

Here's an example of what this looked like once to me many years ago.

I was thinking about returning to the financial planning field to support myself as I was writing. It was a field I knew well, and I knew I would be successful once again at it, but I delayed and delayed and delayed, while the bills got farther and farther behind.

Until one day, the suffering from not having enough money to take care of my family was great enough that I was finally willing to see that a huge "I don't want to do that" was holding me back.

I knew that I would be required to go to New York for a month of training. It wasn't that I didn't want to go; I was afraid that my husband would leave me if I did. Yes, there was a story behind that, but the story doesn't matter. It was the fear of it that made me unwilling.

Once the reason was uncovered, I consciously chose to do what had to be done to fulfill my Intent of caring for those I loved. I joined the firm; I went to New York and had a wonderful month that was full of blessings for everyone, and of course that feared scenario did not take place.

So go back to your "what I want" list, and your intention for the items on it, and take another look at your willing list. What aren't you willing to do? Are you willing now to let the resistance go?

One last thing to know: Often, in fact almost always, you don't really end up having to do all those things; you just have to be willing.

Be willing!

INTENT—DAY SIX

While I was writing this, we moved to a new home. That meant I had to call utilities, canceling some and getting others.

Since we were getting a fresh start, I decided to get a new DSL provider. I had a list of providers who service our area, so I went to each of their websites to get information on their services and phone numbers to call them.

One of those providers—a big name provider that I won't name but you all know it—had a nice Website with lots of information. However, I could not find the phone number to call them directly anywhere on their Website; the only option was to order online without help.

I am an Internet person but I was still not going to order that kind of service without speaking directly to someone to make sure it was what I wanted.

No phone number anywhere. It is a business that is in the business of connection; yet, there was no way for me to connect to them personally. Imagine that!

There is an Intent point to this story.

It is a useful way to examine our own Intents.

Go back to the list you have been working on of what you want—which of course now you can see is actually a list of Intents.

May I assume that one of those Intents is to be more abundant in some form in your life? It could be money, relationships, or health, it doesn't matter which one. Look at that Intent carefully.

Is there any way you are making it impossible for it to occur because there is no way to connect it to you? Or perhaps there is a small connection but not enough for it to fully succeed.

Yes, this is part of the "be willing" concept.

- Look at the practical way it is being carried out, or

how you are not letting it happen.

- Take some time today to check your list once or twice.

- Tomorrow we wrap up all that we have learned about Intent and how to apply it to your life.

Intent—Day Seven

Intents reveal. Intents expand. Intents bring clarity.

Intents, combined with reasons and feelings that begin from within, don't require stress or effort to accomplish.

It is our willingness to do the things that need to be done that allows them to unfold without the strain of thinking we must make it happen.

We can set goals now based on our Intent.

I watched a movie where an injured man made his way down a mountainside by crawling, falling, and dragging himself to safety step by step. His Intent sprang from within. He was willing to do whatever it took to survive, and that meant getting down the mountain.

His goals were tiny. Get to that rock just a foot away, now the next one, then the next one.

Intents are long-range. Goals are step-by-step, day-by-day.

Have you ever biked or run up a hill?

Your Intent is to get up the hill. The goals are to the next tree, to the purple flower, to the twig on the road.

When the going gets difficult, sometimes it is best not to look up and judge the distance. Sometimes it is best to see the short-term goals ticked off one at a time. The Intent carries us forward to completion.

A goal doesn't carry with it the real reason for its accomplishment, does it? It is a means to fulfill the Intent.

Imagine the power and ease of an Intent that begins from the correct premise —that everything is already present, and all we are doing is revealing it, step-by-step.

Perhaps the mountain climber saw himself already down the mountain. Perhaps the biker saw herself at the top of the hill. You are one step ahead. You know yourself as an expression of the qualities of the climber, the biker, and the hill.

Beginning with the premise of One Mind's perfection eliminates any unwillingness, and completes the connections.

Start with Intent, and live in the Grace that is Life Itself.

SEVEN

LISTENING

LISTENING—DAY ONE

For the next *7–Day Shift Session* we are going to focus on Listening.

Maybe we should have started with this idea, since nothing will ever change until we learn how to listen within—to the still small voice that is always guiding us.

On the other hand, perhaps now we can see the importance of this quality, and it is perfect timing!

As we practice Listening, we gain insights, small and large, that help us live our lives more gracefully, and see or recall what we have missed or forgotten.

Once I had to go to the bank, which is about a 20-minute drive away. I got there at the time that I thought it opened, but found I had a 30-minute wait. It was too far to go home and come back, so instead of pacing around being upset, I decided to simply use that 30 minutes to listen.

I parked the car, opened the window, and listened. I listened to the birds, the quiet, and the traffic, all of it without really trying to "do" something with it. In the middle of all that, I heard a voice in my head. It was my dad saying, "Hi, George."

In that moment I recalled a very precious memory that I had forgotten. It had started a few days earlier when I told my sister about a turtle that came to visit me. She wrote and asked me if we could call him George.

I had no idea why she wanted me to call the turtle George, and I filed it away for another time.

As I heard my dad say, "Hi George," I remembered him coming up the stairs when we were children, and the little turtle in the fish bowl splashing around with excitement knowing that it meant he was going to be fed. Of course it was that turtle that my dad was saying "Hi" to.

Yes, a small incident, a tiny memory, but a completely forgotten picture of something very special and caring that was demonstrated by my dad, which revealed a deeper picture of who he is to me.

Listening within, I remembered what had never been lost.

Wouldn't that be just one really good reason to take a few minutes a day to simply listen?

LISTENING—DAY TWO

When I pack for a trip, I take all my trip stuff out, and then pick what I need for that particular trip.

As I finished packing for my last trip, I was getting ready to put away the little bag in my hand when I heard a voice say, "Keep it, you might need it."

I responded, "Whatever for? It is just one more thing to pack." But, I heard the "Keep it, you might need it" voice again and decided what could I lose, as it was an easily foldable bag; so I tucked it away in my carry-on luggage.

Later, as I was boarding the plane with my water bottle, and book in my hand, trying to balance that while holding my boarding pass and dragging my luggage, I remembered that little bag, pulled it out and hung in on the handle.

I tucked the water bottle, the book, and my boarding pass into it, and suddenly life was a lot easier.

Yes, such a small incident. However, that is what our days are made up of, small incidents that we either blow up into big ones, or miss altogether. Then we wonder why, after a time, we feel stressed, tired, frustrated, or depressed—all those emotions that build up over time because we are not Listening to that still, small voice that guides us, with often very practical suggestions.

We are geared to thinking that we need big miracles to prove that there is an infinite intelligence called God. We pray for signs, for help, for the flash of light that changes everything. But, that is a false teaching which hides the every-moment guidance and provision of that Infinite Intelligence for Itself, and we are Itself expressed.

Pausing, observing, and Listening, we find that the awareness of the Infinite Intelligence of Love, or God, becomes an easily understandable and present awareness.

We can feel that divine guidance is as close to us as our thoughts.

Listen, you can hear it now; trust in Love's guidance and provision. It then becomes an awareness that goes beyond faith; it becomes knowing.

LISTENING—DAY THREE

Now that we have begun to practice Listening, we may discover that there appear to be two voices in our head.

It may feel like that old picture of an angel on one shoulder and the devil on the other.

Which is which? How can we tell if the voice we are Listening to is the still, small voice guiding us to the perfection and good of divine Mind, or the voice that only pretends to be us, distracting us from Truth?

Obviously, this is an extremely important distinction to make. How do we know?

Often it is an easy distinction to make.

If the voice in your head is telling you that you are not good enough, not capable, or it is angry, or disparaging, or in any way makes you feel less than loved, it is not God guiding you or speaking to you. Not! Not! Not!

So who is it? It's not you either.

Most of us think that when we hear a voice talking to us, it is ourselves talking to ourselves. Which is clearly crazy if we think about it, because why would we be so mean to ourselves? Why would we say those things? Why would we treat ourselves with such cruelty?

We wouldn't. The voice in your head is not you. I know it sounds like you. I know it speaks in your voice and uses your inflections and your own arguments, but it is not you. It disguises itself as you so you will listen.

If I popped into your head and started saying all those things to you it would be very unlikely that you would continue to listen, and hopefully you would throw me out your mental door.

And this is exactly what you need to do with that voice. Throw it out your mental door. It doesn't matter what you name it, just throw it out.

It is not Love speaking to you this way.

Love does guide, but It is not cruel. It leads the way with Its arm around you, and by walking beside you. It doesn't push you forward to walk alone, and It doesn't hold out a carrot promising you a future that isn't already yours.

Listen, yes; but be discerning.

What voice are you hearing? Pay attention to the one that gives you hope, the one that is loving and kind; and throw the other one out, locking the door behind it!

Listening—Day Four

What about the art of Listening to each other? Do we? Do we really just sit and listen when someone speaks? Most of the time we are multitasking, aren't we?

We are thinking things like, "What shall I cook for dinner, when can I do the report that is due, maybe a new curtain would look nice here, wonder what's on TV," all of these thoughts that go on and on and occupy a portion of our thinking when others are talking.

Even if we do listen, our next impulse is often to fix or comment upon or judge what has been said.

How often do we deeply listen without multitasking or fixing or judging?

If we are Listening with spiritual ears, we hear something completely different from what we hear when we if we listen with a material, dualistic, gotta-take-action state of Listening.

When we listen with spiritual perception we can accomplish two things at once, the perfect multitasking.

In order to use spiritual perception as we listen, we have to actually listen. Not just to the words, but to the meaning behind them. As we listen, we get a deeper sense of what is being said. We get into the heart of the matter.

The word matter leads perfectly into the second part of spiritual-perception Listening. As we listen, we learn to translate what we are hearing away from matter, the material sense of what is being said, and into the Truth of what is really going on.

For example: We hear a story of discouragement at work or home, and as we deeply listen without distraction, we replace the heart of the matter with the heart of the Truth.

We can understand and have compassion for the human dilemma, while at the same time knowing that there is no discouragement in the Life that is Living Itself.

The right idea will come into our thinking, as we listen both within, to the still, small voice that is guiding us, and without, to the person who is sharing with us.

This is the gift that gives in many ways.

It is the gift to others of Listening, and the gift of knowing what is actually True for the other person.

This also gives us the even greater gift of being aware of the presence of the guidance of Love that is always present within each of us, if we would but listen.

LISTENING—DAY FIVE

Can we get to spiritual awareness by Listening to material claims? No and yes. If we listen to what the material world tells us, and accept it as true, then the essence and grace of spiritual awareness eludes us.

If we observe—a different form of Listening—what the material world is telling us, and use it to point the way to Truth, then, yes, it can be helpful.

Here's an example that I imagine everyone has experienced: paying bills and balancing check books. Whether we do it by hand, or use a computer program, there is usually one of two outcomes, when we are Listening to material sense.

There is either more money in our account than we thought, producing a temporary sense of euphoria or security, or less money in our account, which produces a more lasting sense of fear and discouragement.

If we switch the activity around, from finding out what material sense is telling us about our state of wealth, to observing the activity of the qualities of order and balance and awareness (to name just a few that can be attached to this activity), we begin in the arena of spiritual Truth.

Starting with this right premise, then whatever the result may be, it produces neither euphoria nor fear, but only guidance to stating the Truth about our wealth. Our Wealth is permanent, has nothing to do with numbers, and is always present and available.

But first we must listen.

We must listen to what we are being guided to do by the still, small voice.

We must listen to the spiritual facts before we take action, and we must listen to the spiritual sense of what may appear as a material reality.

Listening first, every activity, every thought, every idea, springs from the Truth of our being. When we begin within from this pure state of Listening, we can trust that what may appear as an outward picture will match our highest understanding of the qualities of God.

It doesn't take time to do this; it just takes practice.

Listening—Day Six

Have you ever thought about the difference between Listening and hearing?

Hearing is something we do with our ears; Listening is something that happens within the quiet of our intention.

As I sat on my deck yesterday I heard many animals and birds. It was quite a variety. To distinguish between them, and to understand the meaning behind their sounds, I had to listen.

As I have been practicing Listening to the animals, I knew that the squirrel was telling me that a predator (in this case a cat) was sneaking up the side of our hill.

Of course, a cat wasn't a scary event for me, but the skills of Listening translate easily to everyday life.

Listening within we are aware of what is going on around us, and we can immediately take internal action, as well as external practical action as needed.

As we listen, we become more present in the moment.

We discover that there is no past or future to listen to, or to fear, or even to be elated about.

As we practice the art of Listening, we become more aware of the gift that is contained within each moment.

Hearing tends to be noisy. Listening is a quiet affair.

Take just a few minutes today to sit someplace familiar, and instead of hearing what is happening, listen to what is happening.

Notice the difference.

LISTENING—DAY SEVEN

Listen with the ear that is in the center of your chest. Hear what's behind what I say.—Rumi

As we finish up this week of Listening we are really just beginning. As we practice Listening we will see the practical effects in our life.

For example to get ready for a party at our house, I cleaned off my desk and put away some curtain rings for later. A few days later, curtain in hand, I went looking for the rings. Not only couldn't I find them, I had absolutely no memory of what I had done with them.

Obviously I **wasn't** Listening when I put them away, I was multitasking without awareness. I looked for a few minutes, and then chased away the voice in my head that told me how, once again, I wasn't paying attention, and I went back to work.

Later I got up from my desk, walked to my sewing box, opened it, and found the rings. There was no conscious thought that they were there. I just followed an inward guidance without outward expectations.

Here is one last story that is an example of the power of Listening.

I have a very powerful tiny magnet that I use to hold up recipes when I am cooking. When I am not using it, I keep it on the metal container on my counter.

During that same party, I forgot that it was there and passed a metal cooking sheet pan by it and it got stuck on the magnet.

As I said, this is a very powerful magnet, and it took quite a bit of pulling to release my sheet pan. It would have been so much easier if I could have demagnetized the pan.

What has this got to do with Listening?

We are always being guided. However, every day, all day, there are magnets that pull us to them. They disguise themselves as thoughts—people, events, places, and things—all claiming to have a power that can keep us attached to the material world and its distractions and lies.

It is easier to avoid those magnets when you remember that they are there. However, if one of those magnets pulls you in, there is a simple way to free yourself.

Return to Listening within. This will demagnetize you, and you will be immediately released. No suffering, pain, or time required.

As we said in our first day of Listening, when we pause, observe, and listen, we find that the awareness of the Infinite

Intelligence of Love, or God, becomes an easily understandable and present awareness.

We begin to feel that divine guidance is as close to us as our thoughts.

As we listen, we learn to trust in Love's guidance and provision.

EIGHT

— · —

SILENCE

SILENCE—DAY ONE

I n our last *7–Day Shift Session*, we practiced listening. Practicing Silence is the perfect next step. We often think they are the same thing, and they are not.

When we are listening, we hear sounds. When we are in Silence we are in perfect stillness, with no sound, or noise at all.

When we are in Silence, we are like a clear, calm, and perfectly still lake that reflects its surroundings like a mirror.

In Silence, we understand that we are the perfect reflection of God.

Mother Teresa said, *We need to find God, and he cannot be found in noise and restlessness. God is the friend of silence. See how nature—trees, flowers, grass—grows in silence; see the stars, the moon and the sun, how they move in silence.*

We need silence to be able to touch souls."

Silence calls us all, amidst the noise and motion of our everyday lives.

We want to be silent.

We want to understand that stillness; but how do we get there?

Let's begin by noticing when it isn't silent.

- Notice the noise.

- Notice the distraction.

- Notice the uneasiness.

- Notice the constant doing.

- Notice, but don't judge.

Stay still in your thinking as you listen and observe.
Shhh....

SILENCE—DAY TWO

Did you notice the noise when you practiced listening?

That's the beginning. Now we are going to practice listening for the Silence.

Elisabeth Kubler-Ross said, *There is no need to go to India or anywhere else to find peace.*

You will find that deep place of Silence right in your room, your garden, or even your bathtub."

This makes perfect sense, doesn't it, when we realize that Silence comes from within. It is the opposite of the trance state—of addiction to the outside world and its focus on objects one at a time.

But, for most of us, listening to the Silence is a foreign concept. We may ask, "What good will it do?" or "How do I even do that?"

Have you ever felt disconnected, frustrated, out of control, sad, lonely, or stuck?

If so, then learning to listen to the Silence, and then learning to live your life from that Silence, will dissolve the feelings of disconnection, frustration, helplessness, sadness, loneliness or being stuck.

In that deep place of Silence, you will find the unending well of peace from which life blooms—without a hint of discontent.

So today, give it a try.

Take some time, even if it is only five minutes, and stop and listen for the Silence.

SILENCE—DAY THREE

The world is awash with consistent noise.

As I was writing this, I had heard the distant rumble of cars, and the closer sound of a neighbor with some kind of big machine in his yard, and the occasional plane overhead.

In between all of those kinds of noises there were a number of bird calls, a squirrel hopping from tree to tree, and then, as the morning turned to afternoon, I could hear the loud drone of the newly emerged cicadas.

That was the hearing noise.

But there was also visual noise, and smell noise, and touch noise, and even taste noise. Most of all there was the mental noise: the mental noise of tasks, and wants, and do-this, and get-that, noise.

Where was the Silence?

Even in my silent time on a rock overlooking the creek, there was still all that noise. However, there was that moment when Silence emerged, through the noise.

It was the attitude of Silence as described by Mahatma Gandhi: "In the attitude of Silence the soul finds the path in a clearer light, and what is elusive and deceptive resolves itself into crystal clearness."

We can begin there, in the attitude of Silence.

We can learn to sift through what appears as noise, and hear the clarity of Silence.

Silence—Day Four

Jon Young tells the story of Gilbert Walking Bull, who talked about the training of their children around nature and Silence. He recalls that their parents would always say, "Sh... Sh... Listen."

And although they didn't know what they were listening for, soon it became a habit to hear not only previously unheard sounds, but also the sacred Silence.

When their parents gave them tasks, like finding herbs on the mountainside, they would travel as a group, in Silence. What a difference from our modern world, where our children travel loudly.

In our drive to be always connected, we are becoming increasingly unconnected to the essence of the Infinite.

Unconnected, we work hard to be and do. The noise of materiality makes us feel stuck, lost and alone.

Within the shift of perception, to seeing that all things are present as God only, we can let go of the fear of being alone, and find all that we need within the silent communication with Spirit.

Within that connection and communication there is no effort. Instead, we feel the harmony of One.

As we practice listening to the Silence, we will find ourselves eliminating the noise in our lives—all forms of noise. We will relax into the peace found within the Silence of the Infinite.

Silence—Day Five

It's almost impossible for the modern mind to be still enough to be in Silence. It is so easily distracted.

We are busy planning, and worrying, and wishing. Re-learning how to be still is an art that takes consecrated practice.

Is the benefit of listening to the Silence worth the time it takes to learn to be still? If you have experienced it, you know there are no words to describe the experience, no matter how fleeting it might have been. If you haven't, you can feel your heart's yearning towards it.

It isn't that we no longer hear the noise when we have learned to hear the Silence. It's that what we hear instead is the essence of it, not the material overlay.

In this Silence, we become better able to see through everything that appears material, and see its true substance as the ideas of Infinite Mind.

In the Silence, we learn how to direct our thinking away from the experiences we don't want, and into the ones we do.

In the Silence, we let go of trying to make things happen, and follow instead the direction of the still, small voice, the feminine Principle of Love.

In the Silence, we find the peace that defies the material sense of the world, overrides all distractions, stills troubled minds, and reveals the spiritual essence of all life.

Taking the time to listen to and be Silence results in an overflowing of immeasurable, yet completely tangible, blessings.

So no matter how hard our modern minds may find it to do this practice, let's do it anyway.

SILENCE—DAY SIX

As I write this, the morning chorus of birds has begun. It is a celebration of life. They don't need a cup of coffee to wake up. They call in joy to the morning. They announce the dawn of a new day before it is visible to the eye.

There is a morning chorus every place in the world. Although a different bird begins the morning chorus, depending on the location, it is the same bird that begins it in each place. Where we live, it is the cardinal.

At this time of the year around 5:15 a.m. he sends out one call. To me it sounds like "Hello, Hello, Pretty, Pretty."

Then Silence.

About 25 minutes later, the rest of the calls begin, one bird at a time saying, "I am here, are you? Let's celebrate."

If we listen, we find that within these joyful calls, we find the Silence.

As we study a flower, observe a grain of sand, really look at another person through the spiritual lens of love, we find the Silence.

Within this Silence we can not only imagine divine Mind Knowing Itself, Love Loving Itself, Life Living Itself, but we can feel it.

In the Silence, this feeling overpowers the intellectual process of the worldview and material perception, and reveals to us personally, without anyone else needing to tell us, the Oneness of It all.

Silence—Day Seven

What are we doing when we listen to Silence?

We are altering our point of view and state of mind. We are consciously choosing to be free.

Listening to the Silence can be done all the time. It doesn't require that we sit still for hours, or become mute, or ask for absolutely no noise.

It means we listen to the Silence found within what we are saying and hearing. In quiet times and in busy times, Silence can still be found.

As we practice this skill, we are expanding into a greater awareness of the consciousness of Mind. We are allowing the harmony and grace of divine Love to be revealed to us.

As we unite with the Silence, we are effectively dissolving perceptions that blind us to big R Reality.

We are freed from the confining binds of the worldview. Our imagination leaps into what was the unknowable, and gives us a glimpse of the Infinite Intelligence that underlies, contains, and is what we call the universe.

No wonder listening to the Silence feels so good.

Within the Silence, we let go of will-power, and instead become aware of the qualities of everything we perceive.

We stop trying to make things happen, in essence admitting that we are not the creators and the controllers of our lives, and instead we feel the power of the Infinite One as the only cause and creator.

We experience perfection in the Silence, and that perfection becomes our experience; all of this because we have taken the time to practice listening to the Silence, a doorway to the awareness of One.

NINE

— ❖ —

SELF-LOVE

SELF-LOVE—DAY ONE

F or our next *7–Day Shift Session* we are going to explore
the concept of Self-love. It's a tricky subject.

Most of us know that we would be happier if we did have
Self-love, but we aren't really sure how to get to that state of
mind.

Plus, we wonder if it is right to love ourselves, because we
have been told that Self-love is selfish.

Obviously it is important to understand the difference between the Self-love we want, and the Self-love we don't want,
since it turns out the word Self-love can mean the exact opposite, depending on who is saying it and how it is used.

Mary Baker Eddy said, "Self-love is more opaque than a solid
body."

When I first heard this quote I thought it couldn't pertain
to me, because I was so often "down on myself."

Now I see that "being down" on oneself is the negative
version of Self-love, the kind we don't want.

For the next 7 days, let's observe the difference between negative Self-love and spiritual Self-love, and see what a difference it makes in the quality of our lives.

SELF-LOVE—DAY TWO

Do we need Self-love? Absolutely. Without it we cannot be happy.

But which kind do we need, and how can we easily tell the difference?

When we are attempting to fill something we need by giving to others so that we can have what we think we lack, we act from the place where, "it's all about me."

That is what negative Self-love looks like. It rests in the human personality and ego of self, and, not surprisingly, it does not ever bring permanent happiness.

We rarely mean to make life "all about me."

However, when we don't understand that Self-love is not about loving the human-personality self, but instead loving the qualities of God, present as ourselves, we are always in some form of need, which means that without realizing it, our life is often "all about me."

Jesus' admonition to "love thy neighbor as thyself" states clearly that we better love ourselves well if we are going to treat our neighbors well too.

This is tricky I know. **Same phrase, entirely different meanings and entirely different results.**

Perhaps the first step to seeing the difference between the two kinds of self-love is to begin with the question, "What premise is our Self-love based upon?"

Observe your actions today.

Do most of them stem from personal Self-love or from spiritual Self-love? For heaven's sake, don't judge what you see, that would most definitely not be Self-love. Just observe and while you do, be kind to yourself.

SELF-LOVE—DAY THREE

The Self-love beginning with the premise of a human personality and needs means that we take care of ourselves through will-power, positive thinking, control, destructive behavior (which is actually inverted control and will-power), and hard work.

The Self-love beginning with the premise that we are the presence of Infinite Intelligent Love eliminates need.

In this Self-love, we love ourselves because we are the reflection and expression of God. We care for ourselves within the context of caring for the gift that we are to each other.

What did you observe yesterday?

Were you able to remain kind to yourself?

Did you find that you are often in some form of struggle?

Isn't it odd that struggle is really a form of "it's all about me"?

We all are tired of this struggle, and willing and ready to understand and live true Self-love. Let's give up negative Self-love, and begin to really focus on the qualities of God that we uniquely express. Let's cherish their presence as us.

Take a moment and write down everything that you like about yourself.

It's not hard; no one will see the list but you.

This is the beginning of letting go of being stuck in struggle, so take the time; it will be worth it.

SELF-LOVE—DAY FOUR

As knowledge of ourselves as the qualities of divine Love increases, so does our Self-love. This is an easy love to have.

This Self-love removes ego. It eliminates fear. It dissolves being stuck in negative descriptions of ourselves.

We learn to love and treasure the qualities we express. We give thanks for who we are. We find life flows from this kind of love, and we no longer need to use any form of human control.

Practicing this kind of Self-love is immediately effective and extremely practical.

Here's an example.

Washing the dishes, mowing the lawn, and running the sweeper are all examples of those tasks that we find we have to do over and over again.

It's easy to get into the mode of "why can't someone help me, I'm tired of always having to do this, why am I always the one who gets this done?" and on and on in this same vein.

We all have moments during the day when this kind of thought creeps in and brings unhappiness with it.

If we stayed with material Self-love, then we would feel very righteous with these thoughts; but rarely does this way of thinking produce any kind of positive result.

Switching to spiritual Self-love, we love the qualities we are expressing while doing these tasks.

We love how diligent we are, how orderly, how detailed, and consistent. We love that we honor beauty and clarity. Oh gosh, we could go on for hours with this kind of Self-love.

What are we doing? We are loving the qualities of God, the qualities that we are expressing and reflecting. This is true Self-love.

For the next 24 hours give this kind of Self-love a try.

There are plenty of ways to practice it. Feel the difference between material Self-love and spiritual Self-love, and witness the outcome.

SELF-LOVE—DAY FIVE

Isn't it easy to tell which Self-love we are practicing? In the human version of the Self-love experience, "we need."

We have all experienced this need. It is a need for anything we feel we don't have—like love, money, health, or time. Needing is not a good experience or feeling.

However, within divine Self-love, there is no need; there is only the experience in each moment of the qualities of who we are, present and being, lived as us.

In divine Self-love we find plenty of everything, and our love for ourselves flows to our neighbors equally, without effort.

In human Self-love we ask, "Notice me, help me, give to me, and take care of me."

In divine Self-love, the I AM is present.

Within this Self-love our personality, and ego step aside so that we can be seen as we are: the reflection and expression of God.

Spiritual leader Eknath Easwaran said, "The spiritual life is a call to action. But it is a call to action without any selfish attachment to the results."

Action and lack of attachment are the natural outcome of practicing spiritual Self-love. We automatically no longer worry about results, because our attention is on loving the qualities of God that we are expressing in action.

Self-love within a spiritual context is a marvelous way to live.

Did you practice spiritual Self-love yesterday? Did you notice the difference?

Let's continue this practice. Each day we will become more and more skilled, until one day all we will know is true Self-love.

SELF-LOVE—DAY SIX

Let's go back to that quote from Mary Baker Eddy, "Self-love is more opaque than a solid body."

I knew that the word opaque means not being able to see through something, but with further study, I realized it also means not letting the light shine through.

Where there is no light, there is only darkness. When we realize that negative Self-love is actually darkness, it makes it even more of an unwanted state of mind. Through the darkened lens of human Self-love, we are unable to see the light of Truth in any situation.

However, as we are willing to know ourselves as the qualities of God, the opaqueness dissolves, and in the resulting clarity we find our freedom from need.

We experience instead the joy of divine Self-love, which is always overflowing, filling our lives full of blessings without measure.

It may seem at first that there is only a subtle distinction between the opaque Self-love that blinds us to Truth and the light of Self-love that is the Truth; but with practice we become aware of the immense gap between them. In fact, they are so opposite they can never be in the same place at the same time.

By observing our actions, we can begin to unearth our hidden, and not so hidden, perceptions.

When we realize that the world is the subjective state of our personal point of view, then noticing when we act from negative Self-love becomes a learning and shifting experience.

With this awareness, we can choose to immediately shift to loving ourselves as the qualities of God, and experience without any limitation the Self-love that is Light Itself.

SELF-LOVE—DAY SEVEN

Now that we know how to love ourselves in the proper context, Jesus' saying, love thy neighbor as thyself, makes much more sense. Of course, we will love our neighbor as ourselves, because we see that they **are ourselves.**

Seen as the subjective point of view that we entertain, we know them as we know ourselves. Seen through the eyes of God, where the subjective state is God in action, we know them as God knows them, One as ourselves. Within spiritual Self-love the phrase "thou shalt not" found within the 10 commandments makes more sense too.

Shalt not—not meaning "don't or else," but meaning, "you can't."

Remember negative Self-love and divine or spiritual Self-love cannot exist at the same place and time.

Therefore, there is no way for us to do anything that isn't based in perfect Self-love of the Love of Loving Itself, when we understand and live in true divine Self-love.

Each moment spent in true Self-love erases more of the illusionary boundary lines between each other. Instead we see each other as a unique expression of the One that we are.

Within this awareness there is no jealously or competition. We step completely outside the game of the worldview and see the Truth: We are all One.

This is true divine Self-love.

Ten

Kindness

Kindness—Day One

I was emailing one of my granddaughters and said, "I know that it is not always easy, but if you stick to being true to yourself and kind to others, you will always be happy, and what is better than that?"

Really, what is better than that?

In the last *7–Day Shift Session* we talked about self-love, which is certainly being true to oneself, so we have that covered, right?

Now we are ready in this *7–Day Shift Session* to discover Kindness.

In a study of 37 cultures around the world, 16,000 subjects were asked about their most desired traits in a mate.

For both sexes, the first preference was Kindness, the second was intelligence.

In the early 80's a phrase swept the country: Practice random acts of kindness and senseless acts of beauty.*

This phrase grew into a book, websites, and many current phenomena such as the book and movie "Pay it Forward."

At the end of the movie, "Evan Almighty," God tells Evan that the way to change the world is by doing one Act of Random Kindness at a time(ARK).

So we know Kindness is important. We want it more than anything. We love the idea of it.

But what is it? What does it mean to be kind? Are random acts of Kindness enough?

If God practiced **random** acts of Kindness, would we even be here? Or is Kindness one of those underlying necessities and Principles of the infinite universe upon which all the rest is based?

Let's think on those questions, and I'll meet you here tomorrow for the discovery of Kindness.

*Peace activist Anne Herbert says she wrote this phrase on a placemat at a Sausalito restaurant in 1982 or 1983.

Kindness—Day Two

Isn't it the strangest thing that in the quest for enlightenment the understanding and acting out of Kindness often vanishes?

When we turn within for our own self-enlightenment and forget the needs of others, could that be enlightenment?

Can it be Kindness if we choose the path of renouncing the world, and let others take up the slack we have left behind?

Coach John Wooden said, *You can't live a perfect day without doing something for someone who will never be able to repay you.*

Lao Tzu listed Kindness as the first of three great treasures, and the Buddha taught that generosity is a primary quality of an awakened mind.

All spiritual teachings have strong roots in the ethics of the daily interactions of each of us.

Remember the story in the Bible of the injured man by the side of the road who was ignored by many before being noticed and taken care of by a passing stranger.

Isn't this a lesson on Kindness?

Living the idea of Kindness in a practical-day-to day manner is essential to a happy personal life, and necessary for every person in our world to flourish.

Before going any further, let's take a day and think through what we perceive as Kindness.

Look around. Pay attention.

What Kindness do you see and what Kindness are you doing? What are the qualities of Kindness?

When I was young, I used to admire intelligent people; as I grow older, I admire kind people.—Abraham Joshua Heschel

KINDNESS—DAY THREE

We have asked ourselves what it means to be kind, and we have looked for the qualities of Kindness in action.

Confucius urged his followers to "recompense kindness with kindness." And Albert Schweitzer said, "Constant kindness can accomplish much. As the sun makes ice melt, kindness causes misunderstanding, mistrust, and hostility to evaporate."

Wouldn't it be wonderful if the media and their commentaries were spoken with Kindness?

Imagine how world-shifting that would be!

Instead of telling lies, and stretching the truth in order to be on top, what if we were only concerned with being kind?

Of course, we can not make others act from Kindness; to do that, we would probably have to resort to being unkind. However, we can do it for ourselves.

We can choose not to participate in any activity that is unkind.

We can refuse to listen to, watch, or support in any way any conscious act of unkindness.

We can take action and say "No" when we see unkindness in action.

We can choose to live kindly.

We can monitor what we say about others.

We can act from the intent of Kindness, and not from the need to be right.

We can choose the awareness that it is possible to remain kind and still be wise.

This of course means that we must be aware of what it means to be kind, and not allow unkind things to be said or done to ourselves—even that which we do to ourselves by ourselves.

Yesterday, as you noticed the qualities of Kindness, did you see that some of its qualities are patience, wisdom, understanding, gentleness, strength, awareness, loving, and grace?

There are many people living these qualities on a moment-to-moment basis, and yet it is rarely noticed, because unkindness makes so much noise.

However, we can notice.

Charles Kuralt said, "The everyday kindness of the back roads more than makes up for the acts of greed in the headlines."

This is who we are; let's act that way—not randomly—but consistently.

KINDNESS—DAY FOUR

Let's take a day away from this *7–Day Shift Session* to be kind to others, and instead focus what it means to be kind to ourself.

Why? Because it is so often not done, and it is so imperative that we learn to do so.

The standard of behavior is actually to be unkind to ourselves. In fact, we could appear to be the kindest person anyone has ever met, and still be a bully and cruel to ourself.

We speak internally to ourselves in the most unkind ways, and accept it as if it were natural, even beyond natural: required.

We allow the voice inside ourselves to tell us that we are not good enough, not capable, not allowed, and not worthy.

We have thousands and thousands of unkind thoughts about ourselves on a daily basis, and yet rarely do anything about it. Perhaps halfheartedly we say, "Yes I know I should be more kind to myself, but."

And in that but, the unkind, cruel, mean, bullying, authoritarian, dictator, voice begins again, with its mantra that we are not capable, allowed or worthy.

Just because we know that God is Love doesn't send that voice away. In fact, that can make it worse.

"Yes, God is Love for everyone else, but not for me," we say to ourselves.

Isn't this crazy? It gives us a clue why there is so much unkindness being done in the world. We haven't stopped it within first.

What that bully says to us are those simple phrases that seem to be so correct. "You eat too much; you are wrong about that; you didn't do the right thing; you will never be well; you are required to suffer; they deserve it more than you." Yes, I could go on for pages and pages.

All of these suggestions are unkind. If you heard them outside of yourself spoken to another you would recognize the lie.

Because it speaks within, and in your own voice and inflection, it is accepted.

Tell it no! Begin now to be kind to yourself at all times. Be wise, be strong, push that bully out the door—and never let it in again.

There is no duality—with some people over there and you alone over here.

There is only God Loving Itself, and that is you.

Honor this awareness by not succumbing to unkindness. Instead take action in true Kindness: beginning within. Don't listen to the bully but only to the still, small voice that is God.

We are the leaves of one branch, the drops of one sea, the flowers of one garden. —Jean Baptiste Henry Lacordaire

KINDNESS—DAY FIVE

I was sitting outside thinking about Kindness, and nature arranged a wonderful symbol for me to share with you.

What I was thinking about was the question, "What do we do when we see that others are not being treated kindly? Do we look away? Do we think, 'I am so glad that's not me?' Or perhaps we remain apathetic, thinking that there is nothing we can do."

It was the blue jays who answered my question for me.

As I walked into the house to begin to write, I heard them squawking. Anyone who has ever listened to birds knows they have a variety of ways of speaking, depending on what is happening; and in this case I recognized that they were upset about something.

It was so loud I stepped back outside to see what it was they were so alarmed about.

There they were, the three blue jays that live in our woods, surrounding our resident hawk and screaming at him. They circled, and switched sides, and kept him boxed in with the noise.

He tried going higher, and they went with him. In a few minutes two more neighboring blue jays joined them, and for a time those five jays kept up their screaming, until the hawk must have agreed to fly away, because the jays left and then so did the hawk.

What was happening? Kindness in action.

Those blue jays saw a potential danger for a member of their community, and they protected it. I couldn't see what they were protecting, but it was obvious they were. Blue jays are much smaller than a hawk, and the hawk is a mighty predator, but they were not afraid to face him down when it was necessary.

We could do at least as much for those in our community—whether it be local or family or universal.

Like the blue jays, we can take action within the context of Kindness. This is different from talking about the value of Kindness; this is living its power, and expecting to be the victor over unkindness in whatever form it presents itself and wherever it is found, from within families to governments.

We can be just like those blue jays. Be the first to start, or join those that have already begun; just do what you can do. Blue jays had a voice, and they used it. Let's use ours too.

Silent gratitude isn't much use to anyone.—Gladys Browyn Stern

Kindness—Day Six

In the Talmud, we read that "deeds of kindness are equal in weight to all the commandments."

At first glance this seems like an impossible statement. However, when we examine the depths and breadth of Kindness, we can see that this is entirely true.

If we acted out of Kindness, we would not be able to steal, cheat, lie, or harm anyone in any way.

If we acted from Kindness, we would be putting the Principle of Love first, which means we would be following the commandment of not putting any other gods before God, Love.

It would be easy to know what to do in all situations if we asked ourselves whether what we were contemplating was kind to ourselves first, and then as a direct correlation, kind to another.

Amelia Earhart said, "No kind action ever stops with itself. One kind action leads to another. Good example is followed. A single act of Kindness throws out roots in all directions, and the roots spring up and make new trees. The greatest work that Kindness does to others is that it makes them kind themselves."

When we become too self-absorbed to notice that we are not being kind, we are selfish. When we are selfish, we miss the wholeness of creation.

This is sad for everyone.

It will be sad for us because we will miss the glory of Life, and sad for others because we will most likely not be acting out of generosity, since that is difficult for both the selfish miser and the glutton.

Have you ever proved a mathematical problem by reversing what you did to make sure the answer works both ways? In grade school my math teacher made us do that all the time, and I still find myself doing it in the rare times I don't use my calculator.

In the same way, we can prove to ourselves whether we are being kind by seeing the mirror of life, which reverses back to us what we perceive and believe to be reality. If we find despair, sadness, frustration, unhappiness within, it is very possible that we not acting from our intent of Kindness.

Nature in its beauty is awash in Kindness.

As we are Kindness Itself, we are awash in beauty.

Kindness—Day Seven

Fredrich Nietzche said, *Kindness and love, the most curative herbs and agents in human intercourse are such precious finds that one would hope these balsamlike remedies would be used as economically as possible; but this is impossible. Only the boldest Utopians would dream of the economy of kindness.*

Within this context, I am proud that he would call me a bold Utopian, because I do believe that it is not only possible, but absolutely imperative for every individual not to only dream of the economy of Kindness but to implement it.

In fact, let's go a step further and say that since there is only one Life force, and Its Principle is the Principle of Love, then Kindness composes the DNA of each of us.

Kindness is hard-wired into our system because we are the action and expression and reflection of Divine Love.

It is only logical and scientific that we contain exactly what God contains, and this is Kindness in all its forms.

So when we appear to act unkindly or see unkindness in others, we realize that we are not trying to change ingrained situations or lives.

Instead we are shifting our perception to Truth, and staying there, and as we do so, we see things as they really are, as Love in action.

Within this spiritual perception, all that is unkind vanishes into the nothingness of the missed perception from whence it came. Yes, it takes awareness and practice to cultivate and maintain the spiritual perception that reveals only Love in action.

Seeing and living the qualities of Kindness is a spiritual practice that will reveal the Truth to us and transform our lives, which in turn transforms the world.

One kind thought and action at time. We can do it. We can be bold in our declaration of Kindness.

After all, Kindness is the ground of our being.

Three things in human life are important. The first is to be kind. The second is to be kind. The third is to be kind.—Henry James

Eleven

Right Action

Right Action—Day One

In the world of sales training there was a very graphic sales technique on how to get more business. It was, "Throw enough sh** up against the wall and some of it will stick."

Whenever I heard this, all I could think of was, "Yuck, what a mess."

Recently I heard a very successful businessman declare that this was the technique he used, and it worked extremely well for him. Instead of thinking things through, he simply gets up and does something, and he worries about the consequences later.

As I heard him describe this technique, I inwardly shook my head in amazement. I wondered how he could continue to live in that state of mind and point of view.

I would not want to be like this businessman no matter how successful he is, because someday he will have to ask, "Is this what my life is about?" Then he will have to start cleaning up the mess, and learn how every action appears with spiritual awareness.

On the other side of the sliding scale we have those who have been lulled into non-action; perhaps because they are afraid of doing the wrong thing, or perhaps because they think God will take care of it. In the meantime they live in state of poverty of one kind or another.

The problem lies in a missed perception on both sides.

Does waiting for another person to fulfill our needs seem like what is meant by constant provision and abundance? Is there really freedom in doing nothing?

On the other hand, is it really spiritual awareness to throw things up against the wall to see if they will stick? Do we need to prove that God will take care of the messes we make?

These two points of view, the throwing and the waiting, are ingrained in many of us, and they run the show silently and deeply.

Neither one of them is based on Truth.

Wouldn't omnipresent order move things precisely, at the right time, in the right place, as the omniaction of the Infinite Principle of Love?

So if Right Action is neither "the throw stuff at it" nor "the wait for God to take care of it," what is it?

That's what we'll talk about for the next 7 days. In the meantime, take some time today and become aware of the "throw" and the "wait" actions in your life.

The perfection of a clock is not to go fast, but to be accurate.
—Luc de Clapiers

RIGHT ACTION—DAY TWO

What did you discover yesterday about Right Action in your life? Do you lean more to the "throw" or the "wait"?

Sometimes we are both. Without taking the time to pause and listen, I have often blindly rushed ahead thinking that no matter what happened I would be able to handle it. No matter how big the mess, I was capable of cleaning it up.

On the other hand, I have paused in poverty more than once, laboring under a false perception.

I had once read an account of monks who trusted in God to provide them with everything, so they had nothing, expecting that when they needed it, somehow it would be provided.

I perceived that as a trust or faith that was a wonderful asset and I wanted to have that trust too.

It took me years to figure out that because of that desire I had been living just like those monks, while thinking that I was striving towards understanding abundance.

Because of the underlying missed perception—that trust and faith are proved by having nothing—I had nothing, and if by chance I gained something I quickly lost it. Just like those monks I was living hand to mouth.

So on one hand I was declaring abundance, and on the other I was denying it.

In order to have Right Action we must use all the knowledge we have gained about listening, silence, self-love, awareness, kindness, and intent.

As in all things, understanding, and consciously choosing our point of view, and actively bringing our state of mind into that point of view are all the key to Right Action.

Today, take the time to consciously choose the point of view from which you want to live.

Then actively bring your state of mind into that point of view, so that your emotions and feelings reside in the same place as your intent.

Then and only then will the actions you take be consistent with the choice of how you want to live your life.

RIGHT ACTION—DAY THREE

Now that you are ready to take Right Action, you may have discovered that you are not taking any action at all.

That's because there is a hidden stumbling block that we all trip over. Let's dissolve that one today and get on with our lives.

Within every action there is buried within it the moment of decision. It is the moment we decide to take action or not to take action.

Many people dread that moment, and actively take action not to take action.

One of the reasons for this choice of non-action we discussed yesterday. We know that when we are not sure what our point of view is, and our state of mind is not in line with it, confusion ensues, and it then often feels easier to stand still rather than move anywhere at all.

Today, let's talk about another reason for taking no action.

It is the stumbling block of thinking too broadly and with too much detail. Because of this, we are too confused or afraid to make a decision.

To take Right Action, we must divide our decisions into smaller decisions.

Here's an example of making a decision.

Let's pretend that we want to move somewhere. How would we go about deciding and taking action and actually moving? Break the decisions into small decisions.

It may go like this: The first decision would be willing to consider moving. The next decision is to be willing to decide to move. If everything feels right, then the next decision is the decision to move.

This is the stumbling block for most of us.

We can see that any decision carries with it details and consequences. So in making the first decision, we think that it impacts all the logics of carrying it out, and it doesn't.

Just because you decide to move doesn't mean that you have to actually move. In fact, at this point you may realize that it doesn't feel right to move, and you can change your mind and stay where you are.

Assuming it still feels okay to move, go to the next decision.

Decide that you are willing to find the perfect place. Then divide that decision down into smaller pieces, like area, people, climate, etc.

Take the logistics of every decision as a separate decision, and life becomes much simpler.

It also becomes easier as you remember that making conscious choices means you must be aware of your point of view and state of mind. Then, you are able to, allowed to, and must, change your mind about what you are doing to fit how you want to live your life.

Try this out today. Finally, decide about something you have been tabling for another day.

See how it clears out your thinking and leaves you free to take the next action in your life.

Now that we have decided to decide to break our decisions down into smaller decisions, we are free to take action. But what action? How do we know if the action we are taking is the Right Action?

First, what do we mean by Right Action? In this case we are referring to action taken from within, and not imposed from without.

Most action is not action, it is a reaction.

Something happens, we react. We see it every day within ourselves and in the world. The stock market moves down and panic moves up. We react to news whether it is good or bad. We are happy when good, sad when bad.

Right Action is a response based on the impulsion of Love. We respond with ideas.

These ideas that flow to us are like a direct line to the Infinite. We call this type of idea Angel Ideas. They are those ideas that are nurtured in dreams, and brought forth into action based on the Principles of Love.

It's not hard to know if we are in Right Action or not. If we have to justify the means to the end then we are not in Right Action. Is it unkind to ourselves or others? Not Right Action.

To know if we are in Right Action, we have to be listening within. We have to be still enough long enough to hear those

Angel Ideas, or to hear the disquiet within when we are tempted to make a decision not based on the impulsion of divine Love.

We are all tempted to take wrong action or to react to the machinations of the worldview. Its goal is to keep us distracted and in reaction.

Our intent must be to step away from that worldview and delve deeply into the awareness of the unerring direction of Divine Love.

Take some quiet time all through your day today and deeply listen. Pause before acting, either mentally or physically. Deny reaction its power.

Choose to make Right Action the imperative direction of your life.

Dharma is not what you do, not what you should do, not even what you want to do, but what you were born to do. —Aadil Palkhivala

Right Action—Day Five

Have you ever experienced the *what-if monster*?

Here's what usually happens. You have figured out what you want to do, you know how to do it, and it feels right to do it—all of which are components of Right Action.

However, as you start to move forward, you encounter the *what-if monster*.

I bet it says the same thing to you that it does to me, perhaps with a few minor variations (all worldview monsters are not very creative—subtle, but not creative).

It says, "What if you are wrong? What if you don't really know how to do it? What if you hurt someone? What if it makes someone mad? What if you start and can't finish? What if you really don't want to do it? What if you get stuck in what you are doing but can't get out?"

I could go on with these for pages, but all of these what if's stem from this one:"What if you make a mistake that can never be changed or corrected?"

Of course we will make mistakes. We will offend people, we will hurt the ones we love, we will go down the wrong path, we will make someone mad, we will say the wrong thing at the wrong time, we will buy the wrong investment, and we will start something we don't want to finish.

There is no what if about it at all, because all of these things will happen, sometime.

Does that mean we do nothing? Should we just narrow down our choices and our lives to the safest path we can think of? Even then we are in trouble. There is no safety anywhere if we are afraid of the what if.

Instead, let's agree with it when it says that we will make a mistake.

However, there is one thing that the monster says that is completely untrue. And we knowing what it is, dispels its power to make us afraid.

We can never make a mistake that can't be corrected or changed.

The reason for this is simple. It never happened. It only happens within the illusion of humanness.

In the spiritual awareness that is Truth, it didn't happen—ever.

No matter how badly we appear to mess it up, we never actually changed anything at all in the Infinite Divine Mind of Love.

Our fears, guilt, and dramas exist only within our own thinking. Right Action begins and ends with the right motive and intent of uncovering who and what we really are: Love Loving Itself.

In this place, we have been and always will be innocent.

Right Action begins and ends within the context of the Truth of Love.

Armed with that knowledge, we can be aware of the *what-if monster* and still take action without fear.

Only those who will risk going too far can possibly find out how far you can go. —T.S. Eliot

RIGHT ACTION—DAY SIX

Right Action of course involves doing something, but what and when? Actually we are always doing something, even when we think we are not.

Vegging in front of the TV is doing something. The question is: "Is it the right something at the right time?"

Often in the middle of what I think is something I have to get done, I also have to get up from my desk and go make dinner.

There is a clue about Right Action in what I just said. I really don't have to do either. I could choose not to write, I could choose not to make dinner. But, the days that I make a conscious decision, which is the beginning of Right Action, they may appear to be in conflict.

If I get up to make dinner and wish I were still in my office, or feel upset or angry because I have to make dinner, or the kitchen is a mess, or there is nothing in the fridge I want to eat, or I think how come it is always me?—you know those thoughts—then I am surely not in Right Action.

However, it only takes a moment to shift that point of view and state of mind, to something like this: "I am grateful to have someone to make dinner for. Won't it feel good for him to come home to this food? I get to be creative with what I am doing. I have food to eat. I know how to do this."

All of those types of thoughts begin with a different intent. It is an intent with a bigger purpose than just me.

With an intent and awareness that every action is the expression of Love Loving Itself, then it makes no difference what we are doing,

No matter the task, we can see that we are doing it as God in Action. This is always Right Action.

Household chores are just as important, if done with the commitment to do them as Right Action, as any other seemingly important-to-the-world action we could take.

I often think of the quote by Dag Hammarskjold, "It is more noble to give yourself completely to one individual than to labor diligently for the salvation of the masses."

The next time we "have to" do a task that seems pedestrian and routine and "below ourselves," we could either stay in the "why me?" point of view that produces all those upsetting states of mind, or we could choose to see every task, no matter how big or small, as a chance to be aware of, and present with, the harmonious care and attention of the Infinite Mind of Love.

110

If you have ever switched your perception from one of irritation to one of gratitude, you know in that instant, everything that appeared to be going wrong suddenly internally dissolves.

Give it a try once or twice this week, and experience the shift for yourself. It can and will change everything.

How do we keep our inner fire alive? Two things, at minimum, are needed: an ability to appreciate the positives in our life—and a commitment to action. Every day, it's important to ask and answer these questions: 'What's good in my life?' and 'What needs to be done?—Nathaniel Branden

RIGHT ACTION—DAY SEVEN

In the 70's people would often say, "Everything is copacetic."

This saying made me cringe because I felt that it was mostly used it as a cover-up to not really communicate, and to not become aware of what needed to be done.

In the big R Reality, yes everything is copacetic.

However, that is not the reality from which people were making that statement. It was clear to me that there was something to be done, there was communication to be made, and there were commitments to make and keep.

All of these practical actions can be done within the context of the big R Reality of the Infinite Principle of Love with the practical outcome of more and more of the world experiencing the freedom of being released from the prison of the worldview.

As we have discussed these last 7 days, everything that we do can be done with Right Action.

In Truth we are always in Right Action, because we are the action of that Principle of the Infinite.

To really experience what that means is the basis of all the joy in our lives.

You have heard me say countless times *what you perceive to be reality magnifies.* However, you have also heard it phrased in other ways by many people wiser than I am.

The Apostle Paul said, *Finally, brethren, whatsoever things are true, whatsoever things are honest, whatsoever things are just, whatsoever things are pure, whatsoever things are lovely, whatsoever things are of good report; if there be any virtue, and if there be any praise, think on these things.*—Philippians 4:8."

Mary Baker Eddy said, *Hold thought steadfastly to the enduring, the good, and the true, and you will bring these into your experience proportionately to their occupancy of your thoughts.* —Science and Health: 261:65

This is Right Action. Holding thought steadfastly to the enduring, the good, and the true.

Be grateful for the awareness that we are not the creators, but instead the beloved idea of Love and therefore always living in the perfection of grace.

We can choose the state of mind of being overjoyed with the knowledge that all it takes is a simple shift of perception to once again be aware of the unconditional light of that Love which shines continuously, and without qualification, on every aspect of every life.

This is Right Action, and in Truth there is no other kind.

TWELVE

— · —

RELATIONSHIPS

RELATIONSHIPS—DAY ONE

Life is all about relationships, isn't it? Everything we do involves a relationship—from the clothes we wear, to the food we eat, and the money we spend.

For our next *7–Day Shift Session* we will turn our attention to the Relationships we have, or want to have, with the people we love, or want to love.

Most of us want to jump from not being able to get along with people we hardly know, like the other drivers on the road, to the big relationship we so often call *soulmates*. We think that we will feel differently about being with these special people because after all, they will be "like us."

Plus, we will love them, and they will love us; and love solves everything

Can you hear me saying it? "Not!"

Of course you know that, too. Yes, Love as Divine Love is all there is, but what we call love has been built within the worldview. In order to experience Love as It is, we first must begin by shifting our personal perception about it.

As always and with everything, it all begins within.

This can be a hard idea to face and embrace. After all, those outside Relationships seem to be behaving as if they have nothing to do with us.

Even if we know and accept that Relationships actually are within ourselves, how helpful and practical is that awareness? Especially when we find ourselves in Relationships that are so extremely unhappy or frightening that we can see no way out of them.

In these times, to hear the statement, start within can seem both impossible and futile.

Yet, it's not only true that all Relationships begin within, it is also good news, and a relief. Because, once we begin from within and from the correct premise, the release from Relationships that are unhappy or frightening becomes an after-the-fact occurrence.

What about the other side of this equation—the wanting to be in a relationship, and not understanding why we don't have one?

If we begin on the outside to fix this lack, we end up in Relationships that make us unhappy, or frighten us.

So since sooner or later we have to begin within, why not now?

What might not seem obvious is that even good and great Relationships can become even more wonderful, as we begin within.

Therefore, if you want to give yourself and those you love a gift of a *relation-shift*—it all begins with you, and it all begins within.

Shall we shift together into a more complete awareness and understanding of Love?

The first step in this shift is noticing what you believe about love. We talked about Love at the beginning of this book, and now we are going to expand on those ideas.

What you think you know about love is what you have been telling yourself—and is not what is actually the driving perception, or belief, about love in your life.

How can you discover what you believe about love? By observing your life.

I have always loved mystery stories. I love the process of seeing things differently to discover clues that lead to solving the mystery. Think of your life as a mystery story, and you are the detective.

Your job is to look for clues, unearth evidence, and remain neutral about what you find. If you get caught up in your discovery, you are no longer the detective.

Get in the habit of finding a way to make notes about what you observe during the day. A notebook, pieces of paper in your pocket, or a document on your computer will work.

Observe how others treat you. Observe how you treat and feel about others. Look around you. How do the people you see treat each other?

As you do this, please remember not to judge either yourself or others. You are on a mission quest.

As you go through the day, have a little *statement of Truth* running through your thoughts to hold onto. Try something like, "Love Is Always Loving Itself" which we have been stating throughout this book. Holding to this fact will help unearth those clues.

I hope you are excited, because what could be more joyful then wonderful Relationships.

The fundamental delusion of humanity is to suppose that I am here and you are out there.—Yasutani Roshi

RELATIONSHIPS—DAY TWO

Yesterday, we began the process of shifting to a more complete awareness and understanding of Relationships.

Our first step in this shift was to become aware about what we believe about love in Relationships. We did this because we know that what we *perceive to be reality magnifies*.

This means if we are not clear what we believe about Relationships, we will continue to magnify *our small version* of an Infinite idea.

We began by observing our life, by looking for clues, by unearthing evidence, and remaining neutral about what we found.

We started the habit of finding a way to make notes about what we observed about how others treat us; about how we treat and feel about others; and about how other people treat each other.

The statement we used went something like this: "Love Is Always Loving Itself."

Why did we have a statement of Truth, while looking for what is essentially not true? This idea is an essential part of *The Shift System* process.

Instead of beginning with the idea that something is wrong, and therefore it needs to be fixed, we begin with the idea that there is nothing wrong at all. It is just us living within a misperception of Truth that begs to be dissolved.

The first time I really went on a discovery mission about what I felt about love, I discovered I believed that love could at the same time love me and abandon me. Because of this underlying belief in love, that is exactly what I experienced in all areas of my life.

I could have whined and complained about this discovery. There was a solid reason why I believed it to be true. People would have agreed with me, given my life story. I could have said I had a right to have that perception.

But, I didn't want to live out that perception anymore.

And this is the next step.

Are you willing to give up your life story about what you believe about love? Are you willing to stop getting the secret rewards that we all receive by staying in our human drama?

Most of all, are you willing to be loved and to love?

Even if you are not sure about the willingness part, let's keep going, because, sooner or later, you will be.

What's next, then?

Here's what I did. I started a new True statement. I said to myself, "Love has never abandoned me."

Did I believe this? No. Remember, I had good reason to believe in love's abandonment. But, I chose instead the point

117

of view that Infinite Love is always present, never mean, never unkind, and always loving.

It didn't matter if I experienced it or not: it was True, and I was simply blind to the fact's fulfillment. I said it all the time to myself.

One day while driving around a big cloverleaf on a downtown Los Angeles freeway, I understood exactly how it was True!

I wasn't just saying it anymore to myself, I felt and understood it! Most amazing of all, I saw that it was humanly true too. I saw my whole life completely differently.

What happened? I started laughing, right there in my car on the freeway, all the way home and for hours afterward. I was truly released from that misperception.

I knew absolutely that Love does not abandon. That was the beginning of the end of that cycle of love and abandonment in my life.

So, what did *you* discover?

Be honest.

Now make up a True statement about this discovery to say to yourself.

Don't worry if it feels silly, or if you don't believe it. Imagine what would feel like if it were true, and keep doing it anyway.

RELATIONSHIPS—DAY THREE

So far, we have worked on discovering what we believe about love. Then we decided to give up those beliefs in exchange for being completely willing to be loved and to love.

We agreed to begin and end with the idea that Infinite Love is always Loving Itself, which includes everyone, including you and me.

We started a new True statement that we said to ourselves all the time, even if we didn't believe it.

Did you do it? What happened? Keep going! Be willing to let the Truth about Love reveal Love to you.

This brings us to the next step in this relation-shift.

You are going to discover what you want love to look like for you.

To do this, we are going to put our detective hat back on and search out the clues to what kind of love we want in our Relationships. It's almost like picking a style of a house to live in, but much more important.

It took me awhile to figure out what I wanted love to look like, because I was living my perception based on how I saw my parents' love, on love in the movies, on friends, and of course those love songs.

So I started again, just as you are going to do. I put my love in a Relationship picture, piece by piece.

Once I saw a couple I knew and admired at a picnic who had been married for many years. They were standing at opposite ends of the field. When they saw each other they started running towards each other. She jumped into his arms and they spun around in happiness. "Okay," I thought, "I want that! I want that joy and spontaneous response to love."

I watched another couple negotiate with respect and love everything in their lives together. They were so different, and yet so together, because it was important to each of them that both of them got what they needed to be happy.

Another couple often disagreed with each other, but it didn't change anything about their relationship. They never blamed or whined or complained. They disagreed, figured out how to make it work for both of them, and laughed, and moved on.

Some things I learned because people told me. They told me that love was kind and always available when you need it.

This was a major revelation to me. I had always attempted to be kind and available when I was needed, but I didn't expect others who claimed to love me to reciprocate. I was happy with once-in-awhile: but one day, once-in-awhile was not enough.

These examples should get you started.

Don't forget to write down all this information you are discovering! Your Relationships filled with love should be motivation enough to keep your discovery ongoing and exciting.

RELATIONSHIPS—DAY FOUR

We are discovering what we want our Relationships to be like. We are playing detective by looking for clues, observing love everywhere, and keeping notes about what we've seen, and what we want for ourselves.

We have been studying the love in Relationships!

What did you find? Were you willing to take the time to really observe love? Are you seeing love in a new light?

Remember, everything begins within. Our worldview training is the opposite. It tells us to fix everything outside, and then we will feel better inside. Not only is this bad training, it is a lie.

Trying to fix what started inside by working on the outside picture is as silly and useless as hitting the movie screen when it gets fuzzy. We have to ask the person running the projector to focus the projector, and in this case, we are the person running the projector.

Our agreement with false ideas makes the outside screen of our life fuzzy, or goofy, or sad, or lonely.

What we are doing now is stopping the agreement with what we see, and checking what we believe. We are doing this because there is a law that absolutely cannot be broken within the framework of the world we believe we live in. You know that law as what we perceive to be reality magnifies.™

We are uncovering what we perceive now to be reality, and then shifting it to something much, much, better. All the things you discovered have already begun to shift your life, because it has shifted your perception. You may or may not notice it, but it has!

To have it become more visible you are going to put on your scientist hat. You are going to be a scientist like Albert Einstein who said, "Imagination is more important than knowledge."

Isn't this the same as saying, what we perceive to be reality magnifies?

Perhaps it doesn't feel that way to you yet. However, it will, because next you are going to imagine what it feels like to be loved.

Practice becoming childlike, and imagine what it feels like to be completely, unlimitedly, unconditionally loved. All thinking in the world will never focus the projector of your perception like imagination will, so have at it!

By the way, I did not say, "visualize love." This would be remaining in the worldview of how you *think* love would be. I said *imagine* it! Feel the absolute Truth of it for yourself.

This is going to be fun. It's a time for absolute imagination outside of this world! Enjoy it!

Relationships—Day Five

We have been practicing being aware of what we believe about love, and then decided to be completely willing to be loved and to love. Next, we discovered what we wanted love to look like for ourselves, and imagined what it would feel like to be perfectly loved!

It's quite a trip, isn't it? It's a journey into our own thinking.

It takes us into the past, where we decided, consciously or unconsciously, to believe things that aren't necessarily true. It shows us the history of the worldview, and its determination to keep us locked into duality and lack.

Understanding that our viewpoint is the view, or our perception is our life—and that there is no difference between the two—we know that we must begin within, to shift our perception to the Truth of One, called Divine Love.

This is the shift that facilitates what appears to us as the outside world to resolve into a brighter picture.

It's good to remember at this point that we are not trying to create love. We are not making up a picture in our heads of how love should look. We are shifting our perception to Truth, because that is what we want to know: the Truth about Love.

It is both a relief and a joy to know that Love will also bring practical evidence of Itself into our lives. This is simply like a wake following a boat. The purpose of the boat is not to produce a wake; the wake is a natural result.

Staying with Truth also naturally results in a never-ending supply of whatever is needed, including love.

However, if we get distracted by the goodies this awareness of Truth reveals, it can be like turning the motor off on the boat. The good news is we can always restart the engine of Truth.

This is the main point to think about today.

You are not the creator of your love life, or of any part of your life. You, haven't messed it up, or stopped it, or done anything at all to Relationships in your life, nor has anyone else! Love has always been present for you, and for everyone equally.

All that has happened is that your beliefs and perceptions have covered it up, so you can't see or experience its fullness.

Since you have been imagining what it feels like to be perfectly loved, it's time to choose this as the Truth for yourself.

It doesn't matter if the world isn't showing that to you right now. What does matter is that you begin with this Truth in your thinking.

When we use the phrase I AM we want it to be from the standpoint of Divine Love.

This means we will have to pay attention to anything we say to ourselves that begins with "I am" that is not coming from the qualities of Love.

Instead of having old perceptions be the habit of our thinking, let's choose to make this new shift of perception be a habitual way of thinking, and acting.

This week let's say: "I Am Love Loving Itself." Go ahead, say it, and keep saying it.

Watch what happens!

All perfection and every divine virtue are hidden within you. Reveal them to the world.—Babaji

RELATIONSHIPS—DAY SIX

Is it working? Wait, don't answer that yet.

First, let's look back at our love in Relationships journey.

We have become aware of our belief systems about love.

We decided to be willing to love and be loved.

We discovered what we want love to look like in our lives.

We imagined ourselves perfectly loved.

We realized that we are not the creator of Love, we are Love Itself.

We chose to state that point of view as our personal point of view, by stating "I Am Love Loving Itself."

So, I know you can answer the question, "Is it working?"

The answer absolutely is yes, because if you are doing any shifting at all, then your life is shifting too. There is no way for it not to be, and there is no way to stop it.

So the more accurate question is, "Have you noticed it?"

The shift may be occurring in a way that you want it to. You may be experiencing more love in your Relationships. Or, it may be occurring in a way that you wish it weren't.

You may be noticing that what you thought was love, is not. Or, you may be unwilling to see love in its present package, because you want it to look a certain way. In most cases, all three of these events are occurring.

You are experiencing more love. Look closely and see the qualities of love that make up your daily life. Don't look for it to be in a perfectly wrapped present, just look for the qualities of Love and let it reveal Itself to you.

You are also noticing that some things you called love, are not. This is appropriate and wonderful. They had been here all along and you had accepted them as love. Now, continue to hold to the Truth about Love. Don't get distracted. Plant yourself in love and stay there.

The next step is obvious, isn't it? If we are going to say that Love is all around, and that Love is present for everyone, we must all act from Love ourselves.

If we are noticing that others are not acting from the qualities of Love we must also turn that searchlight on ourselves and ask ourselves, in all that we do, "Is this loving to others?"

I almost hesitate to go to this idea; because some people will think I am saying that to love we must lie down and take it, as if Love is a doormat.

That is not Love. That is not Love Loving Itself.

No. Letting others, or situations, mistreat us, is not love. However, when we notice how we are not loving to others, and begin to actually be Love Loving Itself, then those who are not loving to us will either begin to shift themselves (on their own, by the way) or they will be moved in someway out of our lives (without our making it happen).

So today, be Love Loving Itself. Be the qualities of Love that you have discovered.

When you find that you haven't been loving, forgive yourself, and move on.

Remember, this work that you are doing for yourself will bless everyone around you. It doesn't matter if they notice or not. It doesn't matter if you never get acknowledged. What matters is that your shift to Love, shifts all Relationships to Love.

That's it! You are Love Loving Itself in action.

It's time to be grateful for what we have. This is such a simple thing to do, but something we all have an amazingly large resistance to doing.

Instead of giving thanks, we compare.

Sometimes we judge our own lives, resulting in our thinking that another time was, or will be, better than it is at this moment.

We compare what someone acted like before to what they act like now, even if it was just a moment ago. For example, we may think, "They loved me more yesterday than today. What have I done wrong?"

We compare our love lives with another person's love life, even though we actually have no idea what is really true about any other person's life.

We may believe that others have a better love life than we do because they have—or do not have—a significant other.

We are often in judgement and rarely in gratitude.

I once asked a client to find something to be grateful for, and this person honestly answered, "I don't want to." This is true for all of us. We all hide from gratitude some of the time.

Why is this? Because we know that being grateful immediately shifts our perception to good, and if that happens, it would ruin what we get out of our comparison habit.

However, we can get over the comparison habit. I believe that it is true that we all want to experience the omnipresence of Love—all its qualities in all Its forms, in all Its various and subtle ways—from the tiny to the large, from the seemingly important to the trivial.

We all, more than anything else, want to experience first-hand that the omnipresence of Love is present as our life.

Let's do it, then! Let's choose to be grateful. Let's make now the time to stop hiding from Love.

Take this moment to breathe in and breathe out while feeling that omnipresence of Love. Take this moment to fully and completely give thanks.

Let Love be the essence of your life, without any kind of comparison at all. Let yourself, and your life, be grounded in gratitude.

Love Is. And nothing will ever change that.

Live in thanks now, and experience this Reality.

Thirteen

— · —

Money

Money—Day One

There is no other symbol in the world today that affects anyone more that Money. There is no one who is not touched by the reach of Money.

It's as pervasive as the basic life-sustaining elements of our world, from the sun to the air we breathe. Even if we claim we have no use for it and run from it, it still is driving our decisions. In this case to run.

For those who say they love Money, they may run a different way; they run towards it and sometimes away from everything else.

This is a complex subject, but in this 7–Day Shift Session we are going to narrow it down to a few key points, as we move ourselves to an understanding that Money is neither good nor evil. It depends on how we perceive it.

Of course, Money has not always been paper or metal. In fact, today Money is no longer just paper and metal, it is has become in many ways just numbers, almost as intangible as air.

As with all worldview symbols we must look past what we see, and understand what it is within its true spiritual state.

It's interesting that our Money system used to be based upon a solid, measurable system. It acted like an underlying principle that everyone could see. It was the gold system.

Today there is no underlying tangible system upon which the Money we spend and lend is based. We have come to a place where Money is an agreed perception that has no real basis.

To operate a human system of Money on this premise may be folly; so to try to understand the Truth about Money as a spiritual fact, we must establish a solid principle upon which to build. We must build on our spiritual gold system.

Let's set our gold system then, as we always must, on the strong foundation that there is only One Mind, Intelligent Love, supplying and governing Itself, because that is what It does.

Unlike the human point of view about Money that slides between greed ("I must have more, no matter what the cost") and fear ("what if there is not enough for me?"), the Principle of our system stands firm on Its awareness that all that exists is Itself.

There is no instability, no cycles, no economic swings, no greed, and no fear.

As always, we begin with the awareness that *what we perceive to be reality magnifies.*

In the case of Money, there are very few of us with a purely spiritual perception about Money. We are almost always governed, in some degree, by greed or fear about Money in our lives.

For these next 7 days, we get to practice shifting ourselves to that stable and strong foundation of the Truth about Money. We get to stand on the Principle of One Mind supplying Itself.

Let's begin by becoming aware of what people, including us, say and believe about Money in the worldview.

Get out a pen and paper and start taking notes.

Don't take the easy route and write what you think you think about Money. Instead, pay attention and really notice.

If I told you that you had 7 days to practice for a game show, where you could win big bucks by being aware of the lies and Truths about Money, you would spend the time doing this practice.

So imagine that is what is happening here.

During this 7 days you could shift your perception to a point where big bucks—whatever that means to you—would be in your life without it being either a burden or a savior. It would just be What Is.

Have at it! See you tomorrow!

Let your capital be simplicity and contentment.—Henry David Thoreau

MONEY—DAY TWO

Yesterday, we practiced becoming aware of what people, including us, say and believe about Money within the worldview. Did you notice one key point about Money?

Did you notice that Money is about 2% logic and 98% emotion?

It is our emotion about Money, or our state of mind about Money, that not only drives our actions about Money, but also blinds us to the Truth about Money in our lives.

This means that it remains very important to be continually aware of the emotions we are feeling about Money as we deal with it on a daily basis, and continue through this series.

For example, do you shop to fill a want, a need, or an emotional hole?

Do you feel better before, during, or after spending Money? Are you willing to spend Money now because you feel you want or need something, and are you less concerned about the consequences to your future self?

As we stay aware, the next step is to see what Money actually does in the world.

Once we notice what is done with Money, we can begin to understand the basic qualities that make up what we call Money, and find its true nature. This quest will lead us to examine if it is possible to have something, without getting it with Money.

Let's start with what we now believe we need Money to acquire. Here's an example of this: Most of us feel that in order to have a home we need to have Money. In this scenario Money would get us what? In other words, what are the qualities of home?

Home will represent different qualities for each of us, but for the purpose of this exercise let's agree that some of the qualities of home are security, safety, peace, and beauty. This would mean that Money, which bought us a home, would also be buying us security, safety, peace, and beauty.

Is this true? I leave you with that thought for the day. Spend some time breaking down into qualities the things that you feel Money alone can obtain for you.

Then ask yourself, "Does Money also buy me the qualities that make up these things?"

Don't judge the answers; just observe them. We have only begun the path down the road to the Truth about Money.

We've been conditioned to believe that the external world is more real than the internal world. Quantum physics says just the opposite. It says what's happening within us will create what's happening outside of us. —Dr. Joseph Dispenza

MONEY—DAY THREE

We talked about the fact that Money is 2% logic and 98% emotion, and of course that the worldview believes that we must have Money to acquire what we need and want.

Beginning with the idea of home, we asked ourselves if Money will buy us the qualities of home, such as security, safety, peace, and beauty.

We can play with this idea with anything that we may want or need. Does Money buy the qualities of that thing? Or are the qualities innate within it, which actually make up the wholeness of it?

Many years ago my sister and I decided to visit our grandmother, who lived a few hours from New Orleans. I flew in a day early to explore a garden I had heard about within the city.

As I walked the garden I took notes on the many beautiful flowers and trees, thinking that someday I might want them in my own garden.

The garden was so beautiful it took my breath away, so I wanted to be able to reproduce it for myself.

However, as I took notes I realized I was moving away from feeling relaxed and happy, to the empty feeling of wanting and lack. I could not see how I would ever be able to have such a garden for myself.

It was in that moment that I realized I actually had that garden. Right then, and always, because it existed, not because I had to own it.

If I could actually buy all those flowers and plants, it would mean I would be responsible for the personal care of them.

I knew that was not really what I wanted to do with my days. Instead, I rejoiced in the sudden awareness that the garden was mine—without labor and responsibility.

Understanding that the qualities of what we want are always present, and not something that has to be bought, and knowing that owning something does not necessarily involve personal ownership, is another step towards becoming aware of the Truth about Money.

MONEY—DAY FOUR

Many a man thinks he is buying pleasure, when he is really selling himself to it.—Benjamin Franklin

In his book Geography of Bliss, author Eric Weiner researches what makes people happy. Do you think it's Money? How much?

Here is what he discovered: A little extra Money brings happiness, a lot more does not.

However, we too easily fall into the drug and addiction of chasing Money.

In this state of mind, we are not thinking about what qualities Money represents. Instead, we are willing to give away our time to its pursuit, sacrificing the time with our family, our friends and the joys of living.

As with all addictions, this one does not bring happiness—just more toys. We become the janitors of our possessions.

Working for years as a Certified Financial Planner, I was very aware of this fact. It didn't matter how much— or how little—Money people had, they were not happy until, and if, they learned how to translate Money into something actually much more tangible: the quality of their life. They had to escape the pull of Money as a drug.

There is another side of this picture. Yes, if we work for the sake of acquiring Money, we become its slave. Not only that, if we are afraid to have Money, we are just as much its slave; but in this case, sometimes we can be without even enough Money to at least feel comfortable.

Many of us have been taught, mostly without our conscious consent, that if we are truly spiritual, we don't need or want Money; that if we are successful, we have done something wrong.

This is an outrageously cruel worldview lie that has caused enough suffering.

Declare yourself free.

Choose instead to see Money as it really is. Money is not energy, which can be measured and therefore material.

Money expresses qualities that are the essence of God, Divine Love Itself.

Imagine if all the people who have allowed themselves to be starved of the wealth of God, chose instead to be overflowing with the wealth of God.

Imagine what would happen if we all accepted into our lives the most obvious symbol of God's ever- present Love: Money.

Think of the outreach possible. Money can travel where we cannot, making it a symbol of omnipresence.

Money can be anonymous, changing every life it touches, without need for a personal ego being attached. It can provide items representing beauty, safety, comfort, and security.

However, Money can do none of these things when only seen as a material form that must be acquired. It can and will do all these things as soon as we choose to see it only as the qualities of God in Action, and allow ourselves to receive it wholeheartedly.

Then we will see this promise fulfilled: Bring ye all the tithes into the storehouse, that there may be meat in mine house, and prove me now herewith, saith the Lord of hosts, if I will not open you the windows of heaven, and pour you out a blessing, that there shall not be room enough to receive it.—Malachi 3:10

MONEY—DAY FIVE

Today, let's cover the subject of debt. Debt often begins with the perception that we need more than what we currently have in order to be happy, and we need it now.

This point of view often propels us into too much Money debt, where we spend more Money than we have on hand. It's a disease perpetuated by the worldview as it continues its massive lie—that there is not enough, so we better get our fair share now!

But there is a second part of that lie that we rarely talk about, and it is even more dangerous.

To uncover it, let's begin with Matthew's version of The Lord's Prayer, "And forgive us our debts, as we forgive our debtors."

What does this mean?

Does it mean that an anthropomorphic god will take away our human debts, if we forgive those who owe us? Or is there a deeper meaning embedded in this message?

Our first task might be to discover what is meant by debt. Can it just be about Money? It's not likely that this is what Jesus meant by this prayer.

The answer may be found in the second part of the lie of the dualistic worldview, which teaches us that pleasure and happiness can be found only through material means—and here is the really dangerous part of that lie—that the material world owes it to us.

We ask for everything materially, and believe we have a right to it—from Money to love. We feel entitled and privileged—materially.

If we begin from the point of view that we are owed something, then we are already in debt, whether we have borrowed from someone officially or not. We are in debt to that point of view, because debt is a two-sided equation.

Now the phrase, "And forgive us our debts, as we forgive our debtors," makes more sense. We must give up the sense that the material world owes us, and this will release us from our debt to it.

Doing this, we begin to unravel ourselves from the material worldview's prison, and we will find ourselves free from the debt of needing what we already have.

We will know that what we see, in actuality, is already something we already possess. We will know that the qualities of what we see are already part of who we are as the activity and expression of Divine Mind, or God.

Sometimes we do need to borrow Money to purchase a car, a home, or a business. When we do, it's the intention behind our request and the intention of the lender that count.

Take the time to examine both.

It is possible both to borrow and to lend Money—not from a sense of entitlement and obligation—but from the awareness that Love provides for Itself, and as a result, meets every human need.

Beginning and ending with this point of view, Mary Baker Eddy's interpretation of the passage, "And forgive us our debts, as we forgive our debtors," makes perfect sense. She says, "And Love is reflected in love."

The price we pay for money is paid in liberty.—Robert Louis Stevenson

MONEY—DAY SIX

When we think about whether we have Money, or don't have Money, we are usually referring to a place that we have it or don't have it—like our purse or wallet, or our bank account.

However, since we have agreed that God is omnipresent, omnipotent, omniscient, or simply All, then there is no room left for a material thing to be localized or personal.

Which means that when we think of Money being in a pinpoint locality, like our bank account, we have made it both personal, and localized. So, what we have really done is take an illusion, and made it a solid point within our thinking.

Can you hear the doors of perception slamming?

The more fear, worry, and disquiet we allow to enter into our thinking, the smaller the pinpoint of our perception. Than we become more and more limited in our awareness of the Infinite.

It's a vicious cycle. Why do we allow this to happen?

It's a habit, an agreement, and the acceptance of the blatant, aggressive lie that what we are seeing is material, controllable, ownable, and limited.

It is all perception—all of it.

What we perceive to be reality is reality. What we think is true, is true. What we perceive about something is the thing itself.

This is the truth about Money, too. Money is one of the deepest symbols of the omnipresence and substance of God, but instead we hold it within a perception of limited, controllable, personal, localized assets.

We can sidestep this worldview by becoming aware that it is only our agreement with the perception that there is something else controlling our assets, our future, our presence, and our abilities that gives money its power.

If we stop agreeing with it the whole story vanishes. Let's let it go for God's sake. Literally.

Since what we call God is the non-localized, non-personal, substance of Love Loving Itself, then it is absolute complete insanity to drill down to a localized bank account, and call it substance and real.

Let's make it a constant habit to pause and feel the doors of perception opening. Let's see things as they really are: infinite One as all, and all as the infinitely abundant One.

I had a friend who threw himself out of a poverty-diseased state of mind perception by making a habit of saying about everything he saw that he loved, "This is mine."

What was he doing? He was seeing everything as it is. He was practicing awareness of the Truth of infinite provision, so he could see the non-personal, non-localized supply shining through the mist- perception of human sense.

He was acknowledging that the substance of all, including Money, is everywhere, and for everyone, at all times, because it is the ground of our being.

The ability to do this is available to us all. Let's break the poverty habit by knowing the Truth about Money, and by not agreeing with the worldview perception of limitation.

If the doors of perception were cleansed everything would appear to man as it is, infinite. For man has closed himself up, till he sees all things through narrow chinks of his cavern. —William Blake

Money—Day Seven

My shuttle driver was a talker.

Within our forty minute ride to the airport I learned about his children, his life as a marine, why he drives a shuttle, his desire for a companion, his political views, and, most of all I learned his life view.

He said that he had learned that life was not about acquiring things, or being greedy, but about living each day in happiness. He lamented he hadn't seen this earlier in his life, and that it had taken so many life lessons to figure it out.

We don't have to wait until we are a certain age to live this life view, nor do we have to have many lessons to figure it out.

We can simply choose to walk away from the general worldview of need and greed.

For the past 6 days we have looked at Money differently. We have realized that Money is not a material thing, or even energy; it is a symbol of the omnipresence and substance of Divine Love. It is not localized or personal.

We know that we can be fully abundant without what the world calls Money, as we spend and receive the currency of Infinite Love loving Itself.

We are also willing to have an overflowing supply of what the world calls Money, without the guilt, responsibility, or fear that accompanies Money when it is seen as a limited commodity.

Most of us spend much of our time doing what the worldview calls working for Money.

Even those with lots of Money still work for their Money; it just looks different. However, all of us know in our hearts, even as we spend our days working for Money, that this couldn't possibly be what Spirit had in mind for Its beloved.

Witness the following passage from the Bible.

Consider the lilies of the field, how they grow; they toil not, neither do they spin: And yet I say unto you, That even Solomon in all his glory was not arrayed like one of these. Wherefore, if God so clothes the grass of the field, which to-day is, and to-morrow is cast into the oven, shall he not much more clothe you, O ye of little faith? Therefore take no thought, saying, What shall we eat? or, What shall we drink? or, Wherewithal shall we be clothed? (For after all these things do the Gentiles seek:) for your heavenly Father knoweth that ye have need of all these things. But seek ye first the kingdom of God, and his righteousness; and all these things shall be added unto you. Matthew 6:28–33

From this passage we learn that our daily work is to seek first Love (God) and Truth (righteousness), and then all things, including what we call Money, will be present in our lives as needed.

Since our perception of something is actually the thing itself, let's shift our perception of money from an object we must earn, to its rightful place—as a symbol and the substance of God's Love, Loving Itself, called us.

The real measure of our wealth is how much we'd be worth if we lost all our money. —John Henry Jowett

Fourteen

—◦—

Renewal

Renewal—Day One

Biologists claim that 98% of the molecules that make up the human body replace themselves about once a year.

Some aspects of the human body are even faster than that, the liver and skeleton every few months, the skin about once a month and the stomach lining about every 5 days.

If this is true, and there is no reason to think it's not, then why is it that what appears as the body seems to deteriorate?

Even on a human level, we are symbolically shown that all ideas continually renew themselves; and yet what we experience is at best status quo, and, at the worst, decline, in most areas of our lives.

Doesn't this simple observation prove the error of believing in the intelligence of matter? If we believe the body to be real, made of molecules that renew themselves, and yet we do not see that result, we can easily see that there is an error in the premise.

How can the very building blocks of the structure be renewed and get worse at the same time?

The very things we rely on for intelligence and health—like the brain, heart, and vital organs—are made up of atoms, which have been proven to have no intelligence whatsoever.

When we go a little deeper in understanding, we can see that the body is not constructed of molecules of matter, but it is constructed of systems of beliefs. It is a reflection of our education, conditioning, and training.

We see exactly what we believe, or perceive.

This is true not only for what we call the body, but for everything that constitutes what appears as matter. It is what we call a Frozen Focus.

Using the word Renewal with its definition of "bringing back to an original or unimpaired condition," let's take the next 7 days and renew our focus by replacing false belief systems with Truth.

It's the spiritual version of Replacement Therapy. There is nothing we need to buy, nothing to give power to; it's just a simple replacement of thought and identity from false to True.

It's Renewal time!

Renewal—Day Two

Yesterday, we discussed the fact that everything that constitutes matter is the thought of the thing itself. We know that what we are experiencing as *signs following* is a result of what we believe to be true, and what we focus upon. We called it a Frozen Focus of attention. In short, we can tell what we think is reality as we observe what is happening in our life.

143

We can get stuck on a specific point of view, and live it out, without any awareness of why the stories of our life continue to happen again and again.

We often find it easier to see someone else's story.

It would be interesting to observe the conversations we participate in and notice how many times we fall for trying to change someone else's point of view. While we are doing this, we are not realizing that it is our own point of view that we must change, not another's.

For Renewal to take place in our lives, our intention must be to dissolve our own Frozen Focus by replacing false belief systems with Truth.

This is an awareness exercise that takes practice. Dr. Albert Ellis, an early advocate of cognitive therapy, said we walk around with about 5,000 distorted ideas about ourselves. This means we may have about 50,000 negative thoughts a day, all of which must be replaced with Truth.

We have the habit of seeing what does not work, which is the absence of Truth, and as we continue to support that focus, we validate the result.

We are not *creating* what we see, as in making it happen; we are seeing what is really happening inaccurately—through the lens of our own belief systems.

This puts our responsibility in the correct place, since we are not responsible for something bad or good happening; we are only responsible for our point of view and state of mind. Although this may not seem like an important distinction, it is the crux of the issue.

This Renewal is not about rebuilding, or recreating, or even building and creating; it is about shifting our perception. This is a much easier task, since the end result has already been created by the Infinite to perfection.

Instead of trying to bring back health, or wealth, or love, we only have to take off the glasses of a misperception that have distorted the Truth. As we shift our internal focus to this new point of view, fully immersing ourselves in the Truth and the Spirit of it, what will come into focus is what appears as an outside world, with the perfect provision of health, wealth, and love, to meet our current need.

It's Renewal from the inside out!

Renewal—Day Three

There is a new medical science called regeneration, in which scientists are working on telling cells, muscles, and tissue to grow to make new body parts. Scientists have discovered that cells are programmed to grow and make new tissue. The trick is to figure out how to tell them to do so.

Don't we already know this? Don't we already know that it is Life's Intent to grow?

Yes, these are marvelous breakthroughs in science, but let's look at them in the correct context.

Instead of seeing them as the leading edge of science, let's see them for what they actually are: signs following the dawning awareness of Reality.

The science of regeneration is full of signs and symbols from which we can correctly interpret what is happening.

For example, it's interesting that these regeneration processes take place in a sterile environment where no germs can enter. Isn't this the same as a mental environment—where negative, material-based thinking, otherwise know as germs, are not allowed to enter into our thought and perception?

We often find it easier to believe that it is possible for people to have a change of heart and completely rearrange their point of view with the signs following, then it is to believe that it is possible for regeneration or Renewal to take place within what appears as a material body or material object.

And yet this is the same process.

In fact, it is the shifting of perception, or change of heart, that brings about what appears as a material demonstration of signs following, whether it be an improved life style, or a change in bodily or material conditions.

The science of regeneration is not actually creating the new world; it is the signs following of the shift of perception to what is possible, based on the understanding God as Life Itself. These marvelous breakthroughs are just that: breakthroughs from material perception into spiritual perception, much like the sun breaking through the mist.

We will witness even more of these breakthroughs as more and more people stand in the Truth of Life. Instead of seeing them as a future promise, we can see it as the effect of Truth being revealed.

Embraced from this altitude of thought, we are no longer the effect of what happens to a material body and life, but instead we are the outcome of Life's Intent to constantly renew Itself.

Renewal—Day Four

Renewal. What a blessed word, filled with promise.

We can have Renewal of hearts, neighborhoods, families, lives, homes, governments, forests, gardens, friendships, and even bodies.

One of the definitions of Renewal is the act of renewing, which makes it a verb, or action, rather than a static statement. Another definition of renewing is the reestablish on a new, usually improved, basis, or make new, or like new.

Oh! Re–New–Ing!

Beginning, as we know all things do, from within, from our thinking, from our perception, we could be re-new-ing every second of the day. But, we don't. It's a habit to not renew.

Don't believe me? Just for one hour today notice your thoughts and perceptions. Or if it is too hard to see your own, put yourself someplace where you can observe others as they talk about their lives. Are they expressing Renewal thoughts and perceptions?

Our lives, for the most part, are like an old script. We simply keep repeating a version of a habitual script over and over again. Scripts, which we have accepted as truth, begin with the objective of having us believe we are powerless, individual humans, trying to return to, or get back to, One.

Depending on our point of view, this can either be accomplished here, or only by getting to heaven.

Both of these points of view begin with the wrong premise.

Remember it is the intent of dualism, The One Lie of two equal powers—that we will not remember our divine nature. This lie can't change who we are, but it can hide it from us, if we are not constantly practicing a Renewal of our thought and perception.

147

Begin with the correct premise: that you are the reflection and idea of Infinity. The word Infinity contains the obvious fact that it is constantly renewing. To return to the Truth of ourselves we have to discard the old habitual scripts, one word at a time if necessary.

Watch your words; choose them based on the correct premise.

Watch your thinking; replace limitation with the awareness of Infinity.

With these simple actions, each moment of your life becomes one of Re-New-Ing with signs following, as they must and will.

Just notice! How glorious is that!

RENEWAL—DAY FIVE

We live in a world where we have been trained to want everything now, and we want it to be easy!

We want a magic pill, or machine, or idea, that will transform our lives, our bodies, and perhaps even our thinking, with a minimum of effort and commitment.

In the human realm there is always a flip side to everything, and the flip side of wanting everything now are the feelings of despair, discouragement, and doubt. In this state of mind we don't want to do anything at all because we think, "What's the point?"

Whether we are in the want or the why bother mode, we have let ourselves be dumbed down, until we take no responsibility for the outcome of our perception called our lives.

We think that it is easier to pay money for something that might transform and renew us than it is let go of either version of the garbage thinking that blinds us to the renewing power of Truth.

Every Thursday night, well actually on Friday mornings, our garbage gets collected, and we never see it again. One morning I woke up to hear the roar of the truck as it came through our street. In my mind's eye I saw them picking up the garbage.

But, I didn't envision them picking up the garbage in the cans; they were picking up the garbage thoughts and actions in the lives of everyone on our block. I imagined how wonderful it would be if we dumped the garbage thoughts and actions in our lives as easily as we put out the garbage every week.

It really is that easy. It takes a commitment from us every Thursday night to put the garbage cans out. In the same way, it takes a commitment to throw away every useless idea, thought, and perception.

We can tell it is a garbage thought when it keeps us either in the *want* or the *why*, it begins with the premise of human duality, and it is not celebrating the constant Renewal that is Life.

Today, take the time to collect garbage thoughts and actions, and put them out to be picked up and dissolved forever. Imagine the Renewal that will take place with that simple action. It is actually the magic that everyone is looking for. It is immediate, and it is free!

By the way, garbage thoughts are not recyclable. Once dumped, leave them dumped. Don't take them back no matter what new form they try to tempt you with.

And for heavens sake, don't go dumpster diving, hoping to find them again!

Renewal—Day Six

The word Renewal doesn't mean fixing something that is broken, or making something whole that has become less in some way. This would be beginning with the incorrect premise—that there is something wrong that must be righted.

Instead, we see Renewal as the constantly ever-expanding awareness of the Infinite Divine Mind, otherwise known as God.

When we forget what we mean by Renewal, it is very easy to fall back into the fix or make whole habit, which sends us back to the prison of the material sense of everything.

The question we want to continually ask of ourselves is, "Where have I placed my focus?"

When we are focused on fix or make whole, then we are stuck in a now that is the product of the past, and in a now that is the fear of the future.

If we are focused on the correct premise of All as One, with no past or future, or Life Living Itself, then we are never stuck.

Being stuck looks different for different people. For example being stuck may mean we feel scared, frustrated, bored, depressed, or angry. What these emotions have in common is that they are all based on the idea that something or someone has to changed, be fixed, or made whole, in order for us to be free.

None of these emotions have the feeling of the joy that permeates Renewal.

We can expect that with the focus of Renewal, what appears as daily life will shift from stuck to freedom.

This is not the fake freedom of running away, which is really just stuck, in motion; this is the real freedom that comes by staying within the correct premise and not being swayed off that stance, no matter what the five senses may tell us is true.

Within the freedom of Renewal, there is a lightness of being.

For almost a year, my husband, Del, and I traveled around the country. Some friends gave us a song to listen to as we drove away from a visit to their home.

We played it many times after that, bouncing in our seats with the joy of the freedom of Renewal. You don't have to travel around the country to get this sense of freedom.

Just take the quick trip from the land of fix-it to the constant of Renewal.

Listen to *Beyond The Blue Horizon*, written by Harlan Howard, and Hank Cochran. Sung by: Lou Christie

Here's the first line: *Beyond the blue horizon Waits a beautiful day*

RENEWAL—DAY SEVEN

We started our shift to Renewal with the biologists' claim that 98% of the molecules that make up the human body replace themselves about once a year, with some aspects of the human body even faster than that.

Yet, our primary experience is of decline and decay. Since even within the human point of view we have the ability to undergo constant Renewal, why we don't experience it?

It's our perception, or thinking, or point of view that it is not possible for us that determines our experience. Instead of trying to understand human Renewal, let's go straight to the big R Reality Renewal, where it is never about fixing or repairing but simply the continuous unfolding of the perfection of Infinite Intelligence.

In Reality, what appears to decline or decay is only the illusion of the absence of Truth.

This shifting of perception, or change of heart, brings about what appears as a material demonstration, or signs following. These signs and symbols will appear in the most practical manner, whether it is an improved life style or a change in bodily or material conditions.

However, it is not that God heard us; it is we heard God, and this awareness cleared the mist that hide our current perfection.

With the new habit of watching our words and thinking, we are grounding our perception in the unlimited possibilities of Infinity. We expect Renewal in all areas of our lives.

As in all things, it is a dedication to the Principle of what we are doing that actually does the "work?" Taking one step at a time, and not worrying about the outcome, is always part of the process.

Choosing to not be discouraged at what might sometimes appear as lack of progress is easier to do when we remember that we are not creating something, or fixing it; we are only letting go of false beliefs and perceptions.

Much like the artist Michelangelo when he sculpted, we are taking away what does not belong to the finished product. This is so much easier than trying to figure out how to grow something that is gone, or fix something that is broken; all we have to do is to be willing to see what is already present.

Renewal is not a renewal of material objects; it is a renewal of perception.

Let's keep our mind's eye on the perfection of Infinite Love, and let the rest go.

FIFTEEN

— • —

MANHOOD

MANHOOD—DAY ONE

This *7–Day Shift Session* to Manhood will not be complete until we finish the next *7–Day Shift Session*, which will be about Womanhood. This means for the next 14 days, we will explore what is true Manhood and Womanhood, and also what often masquerades as their qualities.

It is important to understand both, because the male and female aspect of each of us must be completely present, aware, and balanced; and in Truth, it is. However, in the worldview, it is extremely unbalanced, and we can see the results of this imbalance in all of our lives.

We have been trained so long in the worldview of the counterfeit male and female, that the true essence of Manhood and Womanhood is rarely seen and celebrated for what it is: the essential power and ingredient of the Principle of Love that is the foundation of what we call the One Mind, or God.

In the worldview of duality thinking, Manhood and womanhood appear to belong to men and women respectively.

However, in the point of view of One Mind, we can see the equality and harmony of true Manhood and Womanhood in each of us.

Although we may see men and women as separate entities in the awareness that we live in now, in the big R Reality they are One within; and therefore, eventually we will see this unity externally.

This means we can't blame men for the mess that the world appears to be in at the moment, no matter how much we might wish to. It is the counterfeit male, disguising itself as Manhood, that is the basis of the conflict and discord—whether that counterfeit male is found in a man or a woman.

It is also never a person that is the source of the problem; it is always the counterfeit quality, appearing real.

The purpose of this shift session to Manhood is to reveal the qualities of true Manhood, to unmask the tyranny of the counterfeit male, and to shift our point of view, our state of mind, and our actions, to correspond to true Manhood found within each of us.

During this session I will also refer to true Womanhood, but we will discuss it in more detail in the next session.

As always, we must begin at the beginning, which means the first step is to discover what we currently think is Manhood. The best way to find that out is to observe the men in our lives, including yourself, if you are a male. We know of course that what we see is what we believe.

In order to shift to true Manhood we have to first find out what we think it is, and then translate all that back to the Truth.

Don't hide from these questions. This is important.

How would you describe the actions of the men in your life? Don't think just about the men in your family, or work; expand into the community and into the world.

How are the men behaving? What are they exhibiting? Remember, this is not judgment; it is an observation of what is claiming to be Manhood—the good, the bad, and yes, the ugly.

We are cleaning the closets of our minds again. What's in there, hiding out, running our perceptions without our conscious consent or agreement?

Let's pull those beliefs out, and then choose the point of view we wish to keep. Don't worry about the mess this makes, it will be cleaned up, and you will love the new look to your world.

MANHOOD—DAY TWO

Today let's begin with the Truth that male and female are not separate, but One. In Genesis (1:27) we read: "So God created man in his own image, in the image of God created he him; male and female created he them."

There is no division here. There is male and female as One, at one time. This is not a dualist statement, where we are divided up into men and women, one from Mars and the other from Venus.

This Truth means that each of us includes every male and female, Manhood and Womanhood, fatherhood and motherhood, quality equally and at the same time—no matter what our outward appearance may be.

Starting with this correct premise, we will begin to clearly see what has been masquerading as Manhood and Womanhood.

This clarity begins the counterfeit's demise by uprooting the premise of its existence.

Of course you know we are focusing on the qualities of Manhood in this 7 day shift. This is a wonderful place to begin, because Manhood represents the Principle of divine Love. Our intention is to see and live from that Principle, and not from the counterfeit idea.

We are observing the actions of the men in our lives. How are they behaving? What are they exhibiting?

I know we each saw some of the wonderful qualities of Manhood in action in our lives; but all of us living in the earth state of mind also see each day the counterfeit qualities of Manhood in action.

Instead of using the quality of strength that belongs to Manhood to support and care for others, that quality is often reversed—to using strength to own, conquer, and suppress.

Today, let's observe the quality of strength in ourselves, in relationship to others and as well as ourselves.

Is the strength of Manhood supporting you, or suppressing you? Begin within, while seeing the outside world as your mirror showing you what you perceive to be real.

As you spend time observing Manhood, stay with Truth by continuing to acknowledge that all that exists is the Manhood of the Principle of divine Love in action.

Keep a statement like this in mind this week: "I know that the strength of Love always supports me."

Notice the shift in your life from this simple statement of Truth.

MANHOOD—DAY THREE

Have you noticed the strength of Manhood supporting you in your life? Perhaps you saw it in the actions of others or in your own actions towards yourself and others.

Did you see it in the leafing out of a tree, the flight of a bird, a door opening, a safe mode of transportation, a computer to work on, a store full of needed supplies?—you see I could go on and on forever with these questions.

Manhood is easy to see; it is present everywhere. There could be no life as we know it without the quality of support that is Manhood. Our habit of perception is to see more often how strength suppresses or controls. However, when we stop and observe the whole of life, we can see that much more prevalent is strength that is upholding, supporting, providing, and caring through its actions.

The counterfeit male has a drive to suppress the feminine, from which springs True action.

Counterfeit male believes that listening to and following Womanhood, or the feminine, will take away its power, which actually is true for the counterfeit male, so it acts from self-preservation.

When action does not stem from the awareness of One, the only way it can survive is by control and suppression.

This fear within the counterfeit male begins with the point of view of duality and the ping-pong slide of humanness, from greed to fear.

In order to survive, the counterfeit male must try to keep Truth in its place, by attempting to achieve power and control over everyone.

This doesn't mean that this counterfeit male is found only in men. Manhood and Womanhood are in Reality wedded as One.

In the same way, the counterfeit male and the counterfeit female can be found in all of us. Found, and dissolved—not tolerated, not feared, not ignored, not fought with, but dissolved.

To dissolve what isn't true; we begin with Truth.

So let's look at another quality of Manhood and how in Truth it behaves. Let's observe the Manhood quality of life found in vitality and vigor.

Where are these qualities found in your life? Where are they not?

Are there ways that you are unconsciously suppressing your vitality and vigor? Observe, don't judge, and claim yourself as True Manhood in action.

Manhood—Day Four

When you observed the men in your life, what did you see? Perhaps you saw both the qualities of true Manhood and the counterfeit male.

As I observe myself, and others, I notice that the Manhood qualities of vitality and vigor are often suppressed within us.

As humans, we are sometimes shamed or forced into controlling the outpouring of this vitality, the joy that is an innate quality in all mankind. We are shushed, seated, and shut in far too much.

The counterfeit male does this because it finds the exuberance of vigor and vitality dangerous. True Manhood, on the other hand, finds a way to utilize these qualities as it expands into expressing a higher and higher awareness of the activity of Infinite Mind.

While writing this, I watched a male finch dance around a female finch. He is expressing Manhood. He is in the unashamed action of vitality, vigor, and life. He is literally dancing the dance of life. Nature does not know about suppression. The Manhood qualities of life are expressed everywhere in nature, channeled appropriately, but not drugged, suppressed, or destroyed.

Expressing life is what we do. We are Life Living Itself.

Why doesn't it always appear this way?

Remember the curse found in the second chapter of Genesis in the Bible? It states that man must work and work and work and never gain pleasure. This is true in the dualistic material world.

But, we are not material; we are spiritual.

We do not need to live the rules of suppression found in the dualistic worldview. We are the expression of God, so there is no need to accept any curse, because it does not reside in spiritual Reality. In Truth, there is no knowing about or acting from curses of any kind.

There is no fate; there is only Life Living Itself.

Beginning with the Truth that there is only One as our premise and our big R Reality, we see that in each of us is the quality of Life Living Itself, as the expression of our Manhood.

Let it be! Let Life Live within you and as you.

MANHOOD—DAY FIVE

Spiritual Understanding—would you think this is a quality of Manhood? Probably not, but it is! It is interesting how the counterfeit man gives us so many clues into true Manhood.

It's a popular joke that men don't ask for directions. Isn't that the counterfeit of understanding or knowing? This is the opposite of Manhood, which listens for guidance from the feminine.

Of course, let's remember that this isn't about male and female. It's about the counterfeit male claiming to have power. The only power it has is within the human realm.

As we claim and act from spiritual understanding, which is Manhood, we have stepped outside of the human realm completely, so what appeared as real just a second before has vanished.

In their right desire to be free from tyranny, and to be seen as equal, many a woman has attached herself to the counterfeit male, within and without, and taken action from that premise.

In doing so women often become more abusive to themselves, and sometimes even to others, than a man acting from the counterfeit male position might do. They develop counterfeit male strategies, instead of strengthening first their spiritual understanding of Manhood, so that True male qualities can emerge.

When I was young, I often stood up to my dad as he tried to tell me that I couldn't do what my brother was allowed to do. I couldn't stay out as late, go where he went, or do what he did. I would argue with my dad, "man to man". Did either of us win? No. Instead, both of us, standing in our counterfeit male positions, grew apart, and I became an often unhappy teenager.

Now that I have learned how to allow True Manhood to be present in and as me in my actions, I am seen for who I am. Not a girl, or a woman, but complete as One; and my dad and I have grown closer.

The authority, right place, and freedom that women seek is found not by listening to and acting from the counterfeit male, but by listening within and allowing the feminine principle of Womanhood to guide outward action.

This is true for both men and women, as these qualities reside equally in both. As men recognize this equality within, they will find greater and greater freedom from the tyranny that claims to be a man. This tyranny suggests that we must resist the direction of the inner feminine principle.

Recognizing that the feminine principle also resides within themselves, men may also find freedom from the excessive desire to outwardly connect to women physically.

As both sexes identify themselves correctly, they will find that the connections they make on the outside are far more fulfilling and complete.

MANHOOD—DAY SIX

Control: a well-known and well-used counterfeit male quality—prevalent not only in men but in women. It's easy to say, "Let go and let God," but how often do we do it?

Male or female, much of our day is spent thinking that we can do it better than someone else; or that if we don't do it ourselves it will never get done; or if we don't supervise it the outcome will be less than expected; or if we don't step in something will go wrong; or of course that we are the only ones who know how to do it right.

There is no point in heaping coals of fire upon ourselves for being this way, because actually that is how it probably happened in the first place.

Feeling as if there were no control, we took control, some measure of it, wherever we could find it. Some of us take more than others, but except for the very few who thrive in "evil," the rest of us would prefer to give it up if we could just trust that it is safe to do so, and we could find a way to let it happen.

As sit on my deck in the morning, there are trees blowing in the wind, birds singing, squirrels playing, flowers blooming, grass growing, and infinitely more happening than I can see. All of this is going on without my control. It goes on in perfect order, working in perfect timing and in perfect harmony. It is a beautiful orchestration of Infinite Intelligence.

If we make it a habit to notice the constant evidence of being cared for by Infinite Intelligence, and our obvious lack of ability to actually make anything happen (beyond the smallest, in proportion to the rest of what is going on, action), perhaps we would be willing to let go of the struggle to hold it together within the prison of human perception, and let God take the reins.

This evidence of perfect Principle is the quality of Manhood that gives us the peace of mind that all is well, has always been well, and will continue into eternity as well, without any control necessary on our part. This guarantee of continuous safety and security is a natural result of activity and provision of true Manhood.

The awareness of these qualities of Manhood brings with it a glorious freedom from personal control, knowing that control rests only within the only cause and creator: the Principle, the Manhood, of Love.

Manhood—Day Seven

We've reached the end of our 7–Day Shift Session. Before we move onto Womanhood, let's review what we have learned.

First we agreed that there is no division between Womanhood and Manhood, and that it is equally balanced in both what appears as male and female.

We rejoiced in the awareness that Manhood is the essential power and ingredient of the Principle of Love, which is the foundation of what we call the One Mind, or God. In the big R Reality, they are One within, and therefore eventually we will see this in our experience.

Let's also review the qualities of Manhood that we discovered, uncovered, and put into practice over the last 7 days.

We started with the Manhood quality of strength that is used not to own, conquer, and suppress, but to support and care for others. We learned that it is okay to be delighted with the outpouring and exuberance of vigor and vitality, and with the joy that is an innate quality in all Manhood.

Next we realized that Manhood expresses spiritual understanding. As we learn to claim and act from spiritual understanding, Manhood, we step outside of the human realm completely. Then what appeared as real just a second before vanishes into a more complete awareness of the presence of God.

We have learned how to allow true Manhood to be present in and as ourselves in action. We found authority, right place, and freedom by listening within and allowing the feminine principle to guide our outward actions.

We have given up control in favor of the Manhood qualities found in perfect order, perfect timing, and perfect harmony, in the beautiful orchestration of Infinite Intelligence.

In this giving up of control, we found the qualities of Manhood—the strength, life, consciousness, spiritual understanding, vitality, and vigor—present as a clear awareness of the peace that comes from resting within the arms of the Principle of Love.

Sixteen

— · —

Womanhood

Womanhood—Day One

This week we begin our exploration of true Womanhood. Not the Womanhood that the dictionary defines as a woman who is no longer a girl, but the Womanhood that is the essence of Love found within each of us, no matter what age, and no matter if we appear to be a male or a female.

It is the quality of tenderness that underlies all of creation. The Manhood quality of Principle upholds this tenderness, keeps the law of it in place, but it is the tenderness of Love that each of us yearns to feel, experience, give, and receive.

One of the most beautiful aspects of discovering true Womanhood and true Manhood is that it releases each of us to be free to be who we really are, and not what the material world dictates within different societal structures.

Instead, we reach into the depths of being and know that Womanhood is the power that heals, because it begins and ends with Love. It leaves no space for error or materiality to enter into our thinking and our lives.

Womanhood has infinite patience, as it allows creation to appear without the effort of making it happen. It relaxes into the awareness of the strength of the singular power of the infinite intelligence of Love.

Womanhood is the quality of motherhood that protects, nurtures, and releases all into the awareness of the Infinite.

Womanhood represents the highest ideal of love. What a glorious 7 days we will share together as we embrace our Womanhood and Manhood in perfect balance.

Once again, let's begin at the beginning, with our first step of discovering what we currently think is Womanhood.

Observe the women in your lives, including yourself, if you are a female. Of course we will bring this all back to the spiritual truth; but discovering what we perceive to be true is the beginning of the end for counterfeit womanhood.

How would you describe the actions of the women in your life?

Don't think just about the women in your family, or work; expand into the community and into the world. How are the women behaving? What are they exhibiting? Remember, this is not judgment, it is observation.

What an exciting time this is. You are restoring the power of Womanhood for yourself and your life.

Let the blessings multiply!

WOMANHOOD—DAY TWO

As we continue down this path of exploring Womanhood, let's remember the Truth—that male and female are not separate, but One. Manhood and Womanhood exist in perfect balance within and as each of us.

Beginning with this true premise, each of us is able to rest securely in the awareness that we are never without the perfect qualities of Manhood or Womanhood, whichever is needed in the moment.

As we always do, when we begin a new focus, we take the time to observe what we perceive to be reality. This is easy to do since the outside world is the picture of our internal beliefs, habits, and perceptions. So by observing women, what did you notice?

Did you notice that the qualities of Womanhood are ever-present? Did you notice that although ever-present, they are often hidden, mistreated, rejected, not respected, and in some cases even hated and killed?

I know this sounds harsh, but in order to dissolve a lie, it must be exposed. The power of Womanhood, the feminine, is often feared. Why? Because, it is powerful and brings change. Not through violence and the counterfeit male, but by standing in the principle of Love, and by not allowing anything that isn't good to be present in anyone's life.

Notice the result of being less than powerful in Love, or silencing Womanhood, or allowing mistreatment of ourselves or others. Now is the time, for each of us to step into our Womanhood. It doesn't matter if we are male or female. This is about qualities of God being present, as and in our lives.

Allowing the tenderness, love, and beauty of Womanhood to guide the strength of the outreach of manhood will uncover what has been hidden, in order for it to be dissolved in the light of Truth.

There is no effort in this action, because we are not the creator or the cause. What we are is the effect of Love.

We are the Womanhood and Manhood of God demonstrated.

Take time this day to savor this fact, and let anything that wants to imprison your Womanhood to be swept away by the mighty wind of Truth.

WOMANHOOD—DAY THREE

This week let's explore a part of the third chapter of Genesis in the Bible and decide if we want to abide by that story, or shift it for ourselves. It is a story of a curse imposed on men and women by the Lord God.

Before we explore the curse, let's see if the Lord God is the same God that we have been talking about in this series. Is the Lord God the God of Infinite Divine Love?

Beginning in the second chapter of Genesis we meet the Lord God who appears to have very human actions and ideas. He rules, judges, condemns, punishes, and sometimes grants miracles.

In the first chapter of Genesis we met God. This God is the Divine Infinite Principle of Love. This God made man and woman like this: "So God created man in his own image, in the image of God created he him; male and female created he them."—Genesis 1:27

In this first record of creation, God created men and women easily and in the image of Itself, Divine Infinite Love.

However, in the second chapter, men and women are tempted by a serpent to know both good and evil. With that decision, to know both good and evil, began the material reality, which causes it own punishment.

That knowing of good and evil cursed men and women, after dividing them into two separate, and not equal, entities. Having a Lord God cause and administer the curse perhaps made it easier to accept, not being willing to accept that we cursed ourselves by accepting duality.

In any case, here is the curse on men and women: "Unto the woman he said, I will greatly multiply thy sorrow and thy conception; in sorrow thou shalt bring forth children; and thy desire shall be to thy husband, and he shall rule over thee.

And unto Adam he said, Because thou hast hearkened unto the voice of thy wife, and hast eaten of the tree, of which I commanded thee, saying, Thou shalt not eat of it: cursed is the ground for thy sake; in sorrow shalt thou eat of it all the days of thy life; Thorns also and thistles shall it bring forth to thee; and thou shalt eat the herb of the field; In the sweat of thy face shalt thou eat bread, till thou return unto the ground; for out of it wast thou taken: for dust thou art, and unto dust shalt thou return."—Genesis 3:16–19

In simple terms, women have been cursed to suffer from just being a woman, and all of the functions of being a woman will be difficult; and of course, women will be ruled over by the counterfeit male. For men, the curse is to work hard with no satisfaction, until life is over.

This is cause for celebration, because we do not have to accept a curse given to us by a dualistic Lord God who knows good and evil. God who is entirely the Principle of Infinite Good is unaware of anything but good. This means that we can step outside of this illusionary state and return to knowing good, God.

Here is another cause for celebration. Right in that curse it tells us what will happen. That curse—the illusion—came from nothing (dust) and it will return to nothing.

There is no time frame here. Let's step outside of duality, return to One, and dissolve the curse for everyone right now.

WOMANHOOD—DAY FOUR

My daughter sent me a copy of a real article found in the July 1943 issue of *Transportation* magazine entitled, *1943 Guide To Hiring Women*. It included the subhead of: *Eleven Tips on Getting More Efficiency Out of Women*.

Here are a few samples of what is in that article:

"Give the female employee a definite day-long schedule of duties so that they'll keep busy without bothering the management for instructions every few minutes."

"Numerous properties say that women make excellent workers when they have their jobs cut out for them, but they lack initiative in finding work themselves."

There are many more statements that are just as outrageous as these.

Even when that article was written, there were many women changing lives, earning a living, running businesses and families (often on their own), and doing everything this article says could not be expected of a woman.

Is it different today? Yes and no. In some places in the world, an article like this would never be accepted. In others, it is the same or worse.

However, no matter where we live, the point of view that says women are inferior remains hidden beneath the surface.

Dissolving this belief forever means that each of us must fully embrace and live the true power of Womanhood, with the respect and admiration and kindness that it deserves. This begins within.

Are we listening to our own Womanhood? Do we respect, admire, and care for the sweetness, loveliness, and purity that are the power of Womanhood?

Or do we adopt the counterfeit male point of view in order to get ahead and survive in the world? Let's not forget that when we let go of the counterfeit male, and embrace true Manhood, there is no longer any need to push, strive, gut it out, put down, hide, or control.

In order to fully leave both the counterfeit male and the counterfeit female in the dust, we must step out of the human, material point of view of lack and duality.

When we choose the point of view that we are all One, and that we are the action and awareness of Love Loving Itself, we will leave the dualistic point of view that created the counterfeits of control and greed.

As we consciously choose One, we will find our true Womanhood, which is the spiritual bliss of the awareness of Infinite Love.

WOMANHOOD—DAY FIVE

There is a quality of Womanhood that is often both misunderstood and missed altogether: that is the quality of innocence. The quality of innocence supersedes and dissolves the constant worldview suggestions of guilt and not enough.

In order to experience the quality of innocence, not only do we have to stop blaming ourselves, we also have to stop blaming others. Instead of finding fault, we find innocence. Instead of stupidity, we find innocence. Instead of jealously, we find innocence.

It's a quality easy to miss, because the opposite of innocent is the prevailing message that is broadcast everywhere—from the media to our own personal mindset.

Daniel's statement of innocency within the lion's den seems a fable impossible to bring into everyday life. But, he was innocent. He disobeyed a law that was designed to trap him; it had no legitimate power, or basis of truth.

Even though he was aware that a trap had been set for him, he didn't succumb to the next part of the trap, which was to go into blame and revenge.

He blamed no one at all. He found no guilt within himself as he remained with his prayer of acknowledging the "living God."

We spend much of our time reliving all the mistakes we have made. We may think of our huge life mistakes, or our tiny everyday mistakes like bringing home the wrong kind of bread from the store. Within that focus of fault, we are led to believe that we are not innocent. Therefore, neither is anyone else.

However, we are critical thinkers. We question what appears as reality. We question if what others tell us is true. We question the internal voice that brings disharmony.

We ask ourselves, "Is this true?" "What if this isn't true? "Is this the Truth?"

Within that context, we expand from the narrow worldview of never good enough, to the unlimited viewpoint of original perfection. From that unlimitedness, it is easy to see that what the worldview says we are is not the Truth of our being.

We have never left the state of being innocent.

We have never eaten of the tree of good and evil. We remain as we have always been: the qualities of the infinite idea of Love expressed.

Womanhood embraces this Truth. Womanhood holds to the innocent nature of each of Its loved ones, beginning with self. This means that like Daniel, who did not obey the material point of view because he knew only the Principle of Love, we can say, "I am innocent."

WOMANHOOD—DAY SIX

When we bought our home, I was the first name on the loan and on the title. We did this on purpose for a number of reasons. However, neither of us was expecting what would happen as a result.

If you have ever bought a home, you know that for the next couple of months you receive lots and lots of snail mail from people like Welcome Wagon, to stores with all kinds of coupons, and ads for a variety of other things to buy.

The interesting part of it was that it was all addressed to my husband, and not to me. I wasn't even present on the information. This means that real people actually looked at the information they found on the loan and the title, and decided to not address it to the primary homeowner, who was a woman, but to the man of the house.

What does this tell us? It tells us that in spite of the fact that even in the material picture of the world, where women control over 70 percent of the wealth, and make over 90 percent of the decisions involving spending money, there is still a real resistance to putting, or allowing, Womanhood first.

Using that as a barometer of the worldview's hold on our perception, we realize we have more work to do as we relearn how to honor the power and insight of Womanhood.

Instead of giving it lip service and talking about how wonderful Womanhood is, we need to put it into its proper place—first—in every area of our lives.

Let's review together our actions and make sure that in all that we do, we begin with the Womanhood within. Let's make sure that we don't reassign the priority of first place to the counterfeit male—back to the habit of making things happen instead of the universes quiet habit of natural unfolding action.

Let's revisit our commitment to the habit of pause, observe, and listen. Let's stand firm in our understanding of the union of true Womanhood and Manhood as One, within and as each of us.

Then we can never be unconsciously forced to choose the false power found in the worldview of control and domination. Instead, we will rest in the consistent, gentle, permanent, strength of the tenderness of Divine Love as represented by Womanhood.

WOMANHOOD—DAY SEVEN

We have reached the end of our two 7–Day Shift Sessions exploring the "hoods," Manhood and Womanhood.

We have exposed the counterfeit male's desire to control, manipulate, and dominate. Within true manhood we have found strength, life, pure consciousness, spiritual understanding, vitality, and vigor.

We have learned that action is the directive of manhood, and that its direction comes from the feminine principle of true Womanhood found within each of us.

Instead of shame and shyness, we have stepped into the tenderness, love, beauty, loveliness, sweetness, spiritual bliss, purity, and innocence of Womanhood.

Instead of separating male and female qualities and thinking of them as at odds with each other, we know them as dancing together in perfect unity. We understand that one does not exist without the other.

As we discard our misperceptions of manhood and Womanhood, we see the perfect harmony and order of the Principle of Love in action.

Instead of searching outside of ourselves to find unity with another, we look inward and discover that we have always been the reflection of perfect manhood and Womanhood.

Many of us may have found that the counterfeit male has often ruled our lives both within and without.

Perhaps we discovered that for much of our lives we have acted like a counterfeit male. Because this has been our training within the worldview, it would be a common experience for both men and women. So being kind to oneself in this discovery is a wise and Womanhood choice.

As we shift our perceptions to Truth, our past false perceptions, knowing their end is near, may attempt to make us feel guilty in a last-ditch effort to survive.

Seeing false perceptions is the first step to freedom. Recognizing their lack of power is the next.

Embracing the innocence of Womanhood, we can take another step to freedom by releasing it from both our memories and our current experiences.

Step fully into the true Manhood and Womanhood that is the truth of you.

Experience the relief of stepping into your natural environment of the divine Principle of Love—Manhood and Womanhood fully wedded as One.

Seventeen

— ∘ —

Ripe Tomatoes

Ripe Tomatoes—One

Did I get your attention? Tomatoes? We are going to spend our next *7–Day Shift Session* on growing tomatoes?

Yes and No.

On the day I was deciding on the next topic for this session, we were harvesting the Tomatoes that I had planted in the spring. My husband said, "Isn't growing Tomatoes a perfect metaphor for life?"

Well it certainly is. So that is what we are going to talk about: the metaphor of growing Tomatoes and life.

What do we start with when growing a tomato? Of course we begin with a seed. Not just any seed, but a good seed. And we often plant more than one seed to make sure that at least one of them will grow into a sturdy plant.

A seed is really an idea, isn't it? Enclosed within a tomato seed is the entire plant. Enclosed within an idea is the fulfillment of that idea.

However, just as we can't see that tomato plant within the seed, we can't see the outcome of our idea.

This means that we often don't trust that the idea is worth anything—since, unlike a tomato, we don't know what it will look like. And so we often never bother to plant the seed of our ideas.

But first, where do we get idea seeds? Yes it's back to that skill of listening within. Listening within, we are open and willing to hear the multitude of Angel Ideas, constantly present, from which to choose.

Since there are millions of ideas always available (yes there are), sometimes we are not sure which one to plant. Just like choosing a good seed to plant for Tomatoes, we want to choose a good idea to plant into our life. How do we do that?

Tomatoes come in a variety of options, and depending on what kind you love, that's the kind you plant. You also plant seeds that have a chance of sprouting. Hybrid tomato seeds don't sprout.

What kind of idea would you love to grow? What works for your life? Is it an idea that has a chance of sprouting? Will you tend it after it grows?

And while we are at it, choosing more than one kind of idea is good plan. Like tomato plants, ideas grow at different speeds and produce fruit at different times.

Why not get a continual year-around harvest?

Pause often in your life to observe and listen, and then pick a few good ideas to plant.

We'll do the next step tomorrow.

RIPE TOMATOES—DAY TWO

179

Yesterday we talked about choosing the seed, or idea, that you would like to grow. Years ago, I was given some very special seeds from someone's garden.

I have saved them all these years, waiting for the perfect time to plant them.

Ideas are like that, too. We have lots of ideas saved up, ready to plant when the time is right. Of course, we have to remember where we put them; so be sure to look in all those places in your thought where you might have stored something wonderful.

Shall we go back to the metaphor of planting Tomatoes? Once we have chosen a variety of Tomato seeds what do we need next?

Here's a hint:

"And when he sowed, some seeds fell by the way side, and the fowls came and devoured them up: Some fell upon stony places, where they had not much earth: and forthwith they sprung up, because they had no deepness of earth: And when the sun was up, they were scorched; and because they had no root, they withered away. And some fell among thorns; and the thorns sprung up, and choked them: But other fell into good ground, and brought forth fruit, some an hundredfold, some sixtyfold, some thirtyfold."—Matthew 13: 4–8

Yes, good ground—or dirt! In today's world we can obtain any kind of dirt we want to use for planting our seeds. Paying attention to the kind of soil each seed prefers insures a greater harvest.

Planting our idea seeds in good ground is also imperative. Good ground in this case means beginning with the right premise or point of view, which is the ground of your being.

What is the ground of your being? Is your premise that you are the creator and cause and therefore responsible for all that occurs in life, making you way too busy to allow a seed to germinate in good dirt?

Or, have you chosen to live from the point of view that divine Intelligence is the creator and cause, leaving you free to receive and support ideas?

Do you have a barren soil point of view—that no matter what you do, your ideas will not sprout?

Or do you have the fertile point of view—that within the idea is all that is necessary for it to bear fruit?

Let the ground of your being be good ground, ready to accept good idea seeds and nurture them.

RIPE TOMATOES—DAY THREE

We have our good seed, we have good dirt; what do we need now? We need something to put them in. Of course the container could be as large as a garden, but it could also be a pot on the porch. Does it matter?

It does.

The year I first planted Tomatoes I knew that we were going to move to a new home after the Tomatoes were planted, so I planted them in containers. Once I ran out of big containers, I planted a few Tomatoes in smaller pots.

They all received equal care, but the Tomatoes in the smaller pots didn't bear as much fruit or last as long.

This concept applies to our idea seeds. Do we give them room enough to grow? Or do we contain them within the bounds of what we know?

Planting them within the small container of our current knowledge stunts their growth and keeps them from bearing the fruit that they were meant to grow.

Have you ever had a wonderful idea, got excited, started working on it, and then your energy and delight with it simply fizzled away?

Perhaps this happened because instead of planting it in the large garden of life, and letting its roots spread out, it was planted in too small of a container.

Today think back on ideas you have had that didn't work out. Perhaps they just need to be repotted in a larger possibility. The Infinite has plenty of room for Its ideas to grow. Let's plant them safely in that container.

RIPE TOMATOES—DAY FOUR

"Where do you like to grow?" Don't we ask our plants that question? "Do you like full sun, partial sun, shade, or partial shade?"

If we choose to plant our Tomatoes in shade, when they prefer full sun, we will certainly notice the difference. No amount of extra care will make up for the fact that Tomatoes like full sun to fully reach their potential and bear fruit.

Some of my container plants on our deck were easy to move about. The ones that I kept moving as the sun shifted in the horizon did better than the ones that I left in their original location. Finally, I put them all on wheels to make their moving easier.

What about you? Where do you grow best? Do you grow best in groups, partial groups, solitude, or partial solitude? Like plants, no amount of extra care will make up for the fact that to reach your full potential and produce the fruit of your life you must plant yourself in your preferred location.

Of course, for each of us, that preferred location begins within, as our mental state, or state of mind. However, our mental state is affected by where and with whom we plant ourselves. If we are being drained by too much of one kind of location, or too little of another, we will feel the difference.

Do you know your preferred location?

Once again the answer is found in personal observation and awareness. But remember, you have a choice. We are mobile—like my Tomatoes on wheels.

You can consistently move yourself where you will grow best for the time.

We had a coaching client speak to us about a job he was thinking of taking. It would involve a few years of work and sacrifice. That wasn't what worried him the most. He knew himself well enough to know that if he took that job it would lock him into an idea of himself that would last for his whole working life.

He chose not to take the job, but to remain mobile and continue to plant himself in the perfect location for the time of his life. How about you? Take the time to test out locations. And since you have a choice, plant yourself there.

RIPE TOMATOES—DAY FIVE

We have chosen our good Tomato seeds, planted them in the best soil possible in the perfect container, and placed them in their preferred sunny location.

How about you? Have you found your good ideas, planted them in the soil of Mind's Perfection, planted them in the largest space you could find—the Infinite—and then placed them in the sunshine of Love?

On Mother's day, I received a pot designed to hold an indoor garden of herbs. I waited to plant it until fall, so that my new herb garden would be ready when my summer herb garden rested for the winter.

I placed the pot in the perfect location, and forgot about it, thinking it would take many days before the seeds sprouted. I was wrong.

A few days later, I happened to glance at the pot and there were little seedlings everywhere. I had forgotten about them! After doing all that work of the first four steps, I almost forgot to care for their growth by watering and feeding them!

Tomatoes love a regularly scheduled deep watering. In fact, a gardening book says it helps them avoid stress, which in a tomato shows up as that mushy, black or brown discoloration on the bottom of Tomatoes, called blossom end rot.

They also like to be fed or fertilized regularly.

This is just like our ideas, which need to be attended to regularly—not tucked away somewhere out of sight and left to fend for themselves.

Some ideas sprout quickly, like my herb seeds. Have you noticed? Or are you too busy worrying about other things to take care of what you have planted?

To avoid stress—water and feed yourself and your ideas frequently—with Truth.

Since you are Love Loving Itself, this will be simple to do, if you remember who you are.

Ripe Tomatoes—Day Six

Now that you have planted, fed, and watered your ideas, you must be seeing some of those tender shoots beginning to grow.

In fact, by now, they might have gotten big enough that they seem to have a life of their own.

As Tomato plants grow bigger, they start leaning and falling; and if not staked in some way they lose much of their fruit to bugs and rot.

Ideas, not staked or cared for by propping them up in some way, will also lose some of their fruit.

This is also the time you may want to look at your Tomato plants and pinch off some of the extra growth, so that more nutrients can be directed to the coming fruit.

Ideas are the same. They need to be tended to and those extra sprouting ideas pinched back, to allow your time and resources to be directed to what is closest to bearing fruit.

Before you begin pinching you will want to know whether your Tomato plant is determinate or indeterminate.

Determinate Tomato plants are compact, or somewhat bushy.

"This type of Tomato plant is full-grown before bearing Tomatoes, and has a predetermined number of stems, leaves, and flowers hardwired into their genetic structure," says Frank

Ferrandino in Kitchen Gardener. "The development of these plants follows a well-defined pattern."

Of course, with this type of Tomato there is no pruning necessary; and if you did, you would have no Tomatoes.

There are some ideas that are the same way.

They have a predetermined life and structure. No pruning necessary. Pay attention, and it will be obvious which is which.

For those Tomatoes that do need to be pruned or pinched, you could actually root some of the shoots that you have pinched off and grow a new plant.

Again, in the same way, when you pinch back one of your current ideas, those smaller ideas can be re-rooted to grow into another stand-alone idea for later.

This way you have a continuing source of fruit- bearing Tomatoes, and ideas, to feed you and your loved ones for a long time.

Though they appear to be separate tasks, pruning and staking truly go together.

If you prune your plants, and wonderful Tomatoes appear, but the plants are not staked, you have wasted your time.

Of course, you could choose not to prune or stake your ideas, or Tomatoes—if you are willing to settle for less than the best possible outcome.

But, with all the care you have taken so far, why stop now?

RIPE TOMATOES—DAY SEVEN

For the past 7 days, we have found the perfect seeds for our Tomatoes—and our ideas. We provided them with the best soil, found wonderful containers, located them in the sunlight of love, watered them, fed them, cared for them by staking and pruning, and now we are ready.

Okay, actually it takes longer than 7 days to take a Tomato from seed to fruit; and of course ideas can take many weeks, months, and years to grow from an idea to fruition.

But the concept is clear. Pick what you have grown, or it will rot.

This sounds like one of those duh statements, but it happens so often that it is more like a geez statement.

We are so busy just doing tasks that we often forget to check our Tomatoes and ideas—to see if they are bearing or have borne fruit.

We are so caught up in the details of life that we are blind to the joys of life.

We are so programmed to think that the time for our reward is sometime in the future, we forget that in every moment there is a harvest.

Jesus said, "Say not ye, There are yet four months, and then cometh harvest, behold, I say unto you, Lift up your eyes, and look on the fields; for they are white already to harvest."—John 4: 35

Yes, in every moment the fields are ripe already for the harvest. There is joy, love, patience, and happiness to be found in each breath. Ideas do bear fruit. The acorn does grow into a tree. We are always supplied; there is always a harvest.

Look now. Get quiet for a moment, breath in, breath out, and experience what is present now for you to savor.

Our role is to take action as led by the still, small voice and to enjoy, but not to create.

That's been done for us. We just have to pause, observe, and listen more often to be aware of it.

Do that now, and feel the harvest that is waiting for you!

EIGHTEEN

—— • ——

RIGHT THINKING

RIGHT THINKING—DAY ONE

L et's spend our last 7 days together doing the most important thing we can do, shift our normal everyday thinking
to Right Thinking. There are *7 Steps to Right Thinking*, which
is perfect for our 7 days together.

After all these shifts together we are most certainly ready
for this subject! Our spiritual muscles have been built up and
made strong, and we are now ready to leave a habitual material
perception for a constant spiritual perception.

We can stop living as if there were two worlds, and choose to
live in big R Reality.

The disciples had a Pentecostal experience as they were all
in one accord in one place. They were filled with the Holy
Ghost, or the spirit of awareness of God. They were one in the
recognition of the Divine Reality.

We can experience this too, as we gather in one accord in one
place (Right Thinking). We can be filled with the awareness of
God. We can live in the recognition of Divine Reality.

We begin with the first step of Right Intent. We covered this briefly at the beginning of the book. Let's look more deeply at it today.

We know that we have to begin with Right Intent in order for everything else to be grounded in the correct principle.

Do you know your Intent in each thought and action? Is it grounded in the first commandment of "Thou shalt have no other Gods before me"?

Years ago, I discovered a prayer that helps me establish my Intent in every action, but especially in the ones I am afraid to do, or don't want to do, which, not surprisingly, are often the same thing.

It is part of a poem written by Mary Baker Eddy and it goes like this, "...my prayer, some daily good to do for Thine, for Thee; and offering pure of Love whereto God leadeth me."

This kind of prayer is about desiring an Intent that is in line with spiritual perception.

We are not asking for something from a human-like god, we are starting with the Intent to act as God's expression.

What a great place to start!

So today, let's be sure we are thinking and acting from pure Right Intent. Of course, to do this, we'll need to pull in all our perception skills.

Pause often. Observe without judgment. Listen deeply.

RIGHT THINKING—DAY TWO

Yesterday, we began by practicing Right Intent. Without stopping that practice, let's continue to the next R in the *7 Steps To Right Thinking:* Right Premise.

In The Shift® we always refer to the two modes of perception: point of view and state of mind. With Right Premise, we are choosing the point of view of One as our Premise.

It's easy to say we are all One, but what does that mean? All One what? Or said another way, One with what? Do we mean we are one with each other, or One with the One?

It important to be clear what Premise we are beginning with as our point of view, isn't it?

Since everything flows from our Intent and Premise, we must know what we believe to be the ground of our being, the force or intelligence of what we see as life.

It doesn't matter what we call this Divine Intelligence, but God is the name that many people know.

I like using this word for the Divine Intelligence since the word God comes from the word good.

I made up an acronym for the word God, *Guarantee of Delivery.*

An omnipresent, omnipotent, omniscient, omniaction God always delivers. It also goes along with the law that *what you perceive to be reality magnifies.* It is a guarantee of delivery.

Since God is All-Good, then there is a guarantee of the delivery of all-good.

However, if we begin with a premise other than God as Infinite Good, our life won't always deliver good.

Instead, it will deliver garbage—the amount and quality of which will be in direct correlation to our missed perception of God.

Therefore, it is imperative to think and act from the Right Premise as God and as our Right Intent.

191

Mary Baker Eddy's definition of God is: "The great I AM, the all-knowing, all-seeing, all-acting, all-wise, all-loving, and eternal; Principle; Mind; Soul; Spirit; Live; Truth; Love; all substance; intelligence."

Applying these 7 Synonyms for God to our thinking gives us a good litmus test to discover if we are acting from the Right Premise.

It will also make clear how we are One.

RIGHT THINKING—DAY THREE

We have covered the first two steps of Right Thinking—Right Intent and Right Premise—which leads us logically to the next step: Right Identity.

When I have an idea about doing something expansive, I sometimes hear a worldview voice that says, "Just who do you think you are?"

I am sure that you have heard it, too.

As we attempt something new in thought, or action, that voice pops up and attempts to stop us in our tracks.

If we are not awake and aware, it freezes us in place for many more moments than are necessary. Sometimes years or even lifetimes pass before we gain the wisdom and courage to answer correctly.

You are at the point now where you have the wisdom and courage to answer, "I am the active expression and reflection of the Infinite Intelligence of the Divine Mind of Love."

Man (as in mankind) is the reflection, or manifestation, of God.

Each of us reflects, in consciousness, all the qualities of God, individualized as our true selfhood.

This is the Christ-consciousness, yours and mine, which we declare as Truth. And from that Principle of Truth we find our Right Identity.

We are not our personality. We are not our history. We are not the stories that we have told about ourselves, no matter how many times we have told them, or how many people believe them.

Looking past what appears to be material, we see the spiritual nature of man and the universe—including us!

So when that voice says, "Just who do you think you are?" we answer without reservation or hesitation, "I am the presence of that I AM."

No man has a prosperity so high or firm, but that two or three words can dishearten it; and there is no calamity which right words will not begin to redress.—Ralph Waldo Emerson

RIGHT THINKING—DAY FOUR

Today is an important day. Today we learn about Right Resistance.

It sounds strange doesn't it? We spend so much time learning not to resist; why spend time learning how to resist? The key to understanding this is to know what, and when, to resist.

Of course, we don't want to resist the infinite divine impulsion of Love at any time.

We always want to yield to the One guiding Principle in every aspect of our lives.

However, our worldview training is exactly the opposite. We have been taught to resist good and let evil alone.

Now that we have begun to learn how not to resist good, it is time to learn how not to let evil alone, but to discern what it is, resist its compulsion in our lives, and forever dissolve its power to destroy lives.

Before proceeding, let's define what we are calling evil. I am using this definition from Ann Beals: A universal incorporeal mental force in human existence claiming to be a hypnotic power opposed to God.

Note the word human and the word claiming. As we stand completely with the Truth—that we are spiritual beings—we have already stepped outside of the agreement, and the assumed power, of evil.

However, until we are completely aware of Truth, and living It all of the time, we must pay attention to what this hypnotic power is attempting to do. Why? Because it is compulsively aggressive, and uses fear as control. It applies the devil's favorite tool of doubt at every opportunity.

Right Resistance is about resisting any form of this lie, and dissolving it with Truth.

We say, "No" to its various forms—like hypnotic states, depression, sickness, lack, discord, irritation, resentment, grief, sensualism, loneliness, and human personality traits.

We do this by adhering to and living within the Principles of the Infinite Intelligence of the Mind of Love.

This decisive resistance, which is not running away from, but standing in Truth, will dissolve all that is unlike Good, or God.

The lie of evil is one lie. It is the lie that there are two powers, good and evil. Both cannot be in the same place at the same time.

In Right Resistance we stand in good, and thus dissolve the dualistic lie of evil in whatever form in which it attempts to masquerade.

In Tom Brown's book, Vision, he quotes the man he calls Grandfather, as saying, "Grandson, a true warrior is the last one to pick up the lance or go to battle. His battles are fought with the lance of love and understanding. His enemies are prejudice, greed and bad medicine, and the biggest battles are always fought within himself. So do not go out upon the earth to battle unseen demons of the physical world, for your hatred will be like theirs. Instead, go out as a true warrior, with love and understanding."

Start to notice how often you decide to not resist evil.

Decide instead to be a true warrior for Truth.

Take up the sword of Love and understanding, which is Right Resistance.

I am not only a pacifist but a militant pacifist. I am willing to fight for peace.—Albert Einstein

RIGHT THINKING—DAY FIVE

Now that we have applied Right Resistance, we can move to the next step in Right Thinking, the R of Right Reasoning.

The hard part is behind us. Now we can stand in the actual Truth of our being. This awareness of Truth is what heals, appearing as healing. In reality, it is simply the uncovering of what is already True, the perfectness of the Infinite. We are never healing or fixing; we are discovering the perfection of God.

This is the step where we apply logic. Not the logic of trying to make old habits and beliefs fit into what we want them to mean within the Infinite.

Instead we are applying the logic that says because the Infinite is omnipresent, omniscient, omniaction, and omnipotent, there is absolutely no room for two powers.

Only one can exist. Which one? Infinite Good, or infinite evil?

Let's assume we cannot figure out the answer to this question yet. We are not sure. We have doubt.

This is where Right Reasoning comes in handy.

If we begin with what we know to be true—that *what we perceive to be reality magnifies*—we know that whichever power we pick is what we will live with.

If we decide that there are two powers, then we are not agreeing that there is an Infinite One; we have stated instead that there is duality.

Then, that's exactly what we'll get; duality. Life will be sometimes good, sometimes bad, never safe, and always confusing.

As we make the decision to choose the point of view that there is an infinite One, which one shall we pick? Good or evil?

Perhaps we need to discover which one will win, and take that side.

Once again, exercise your Right Reasoning. Look around. Evil makes a lot of noise. It is promoted at every opportunity. But which one wins in the end? Good or evil?

I know which one I choose. I know which one wins, because I have reasoned it through.

Take some time and see which one you think wins. And then, ask yourself if you have thoroughly chosen that side, or if you have been walking the dualistic line.

We all do sometimes. We all must stop sometime. Why not now?

Right Thinking—Day Six

If you have ever taken any kind of lesson—like music, dance, sports, or art—you have been taught Right Practice, the next R in the *7 Steps of Right Thinking*.

You were taught that practice makes perfect. You learned that you have to practice the basic principles over and over again in order to be a master at what you are doing.

In every discipline there is a basic core that must be repeated, no matter how many years we have been doing it. Piano players play scales, ballet dancers do a daily barre, golfers practice their swing and their puts.

No matter how good we get at what we are doing, we are always a student of it, if we want to keep gathering every last drop of the essence of what the discipline has to offer.

So even though we may be doing the same movement that we did yesterday, the same scales, or the same swing, if we are paying attention, we notice that it is always different. We are in a different state of mind each day. If we have been practicing, we are also living with a different skill set. Practicing makes us present in what we are doing.

If you have practiced something over and over again, you have also probably experienced that moment when something "clicked" and everything shifted into place, and then a new view of what you had heard before became clear.

This clarity shifts everything, not just what you have been practicing, but everything.

It's as if you stepped into a brand new world; and in essence that is exactly what happened.

It seems obvious, doesn't it? The worldview, or that which does not want us to remember who we are and does not want us to figure out that it is putting forth an illusion (because then it will simply dissolve into its nothingness) will do anything at all to distract us from practicing Truth.

Right Practice is the Repetition of what we have heard or known before. It is reading it again, listening again, and studying again. Being a student of Truth, like all disciplines, is Repetition and practice.

When I lived in Santa Monica, California, I knew a woman who ran three miles every day down to the beach and back. She told me that many people said to her, "Oh, I could do that.

She would invite them to join her—and some did for a day or two–but then they would not come back. Soon she would answer those who said, "I could do that" by asking, "But could you do it every day?"

That's the true sign of a student who desires to know the subject. Not going for the quick high from doing something once, but for the love of the learning and doing—for the pleasure in the knowledge that repetition and practice build a basis that can never be undone.

The student of Truth receives even more pleasure, because every day brings clarity and peace and strength—built on the Principle of Love.

The result is stated perfectly in the Bible passage, *For now we see through a glass, darkly; but then face to face: now I know in part; but then shall I know even as also I am known.*—I Corinthians 13:12

To know as we are known by the Divine. I can't think of anything more wonderful than that, can you?

RIGHT THINKING—DAY SEVEN

As we finish up our *7 Steps To Right Thinking,* it is appropriate to end with Right Action.

We have everything in place in order to take Right Action. Perhaps this is the most important step: taking action. Otherwise, all that we have learned is simply theoretical and impractical.

American Indians are well known for their point of view: that all action takes place only after having a clear Intent on how it will affect 7 generations.

This Intent springs from a deep understanding of the interconnection of everything, and the knowledge that every action we take sends concentric rings outward that continue, and continue, and continue.

When we take action from Right Intent, this is good news, because it means we don't have to look for the result of what we do to know whether or not we have done the right thing. Sometimes results are not immediately seen. Instead, we can rest in the awareness that the effect will remain forever, and we can turn our attention to continuing to do the right thing.

Martin Luther King, Jr. said, *Cowardice asks the question, 'Is it safe?' Expediency asks the question, 'Is it politic?' Vanity asks the question, 'Is it popular?' But, conscience asks the question, 'Is it right?' And there comes a time when one must take a position that is neither safe, nor politic, nor popular, but one must take it because one's conscience tells one that it is right.*

Before taking action of any kind, pause. Ask yourself, "Have I tried it this way before? Did I have the same point of view before? Am I in the same state of mind that I was in before?"

If you have answered "yes" to any of these questions, it is best to not take action yet. Reset your point of view to your current highest understanding of the divine Infinite Mind of Love. Then reset your state of mind to calmness and awareness of the power of that point of view.

Listen deeply to hear direction from the feminine voice within, the power of true Womanhood; then, and only then, take action using the power of true Manhood that exists within.

Albert Einstein defined insanity as "doing the same thing over and over again and expecting different results." He also said, "The only real valuable thing is intuition," and "The true sign of intelligence is not knowledge, but imagination."

Put these three ideas together, and we have Right Action.

And as we gather together all that we have learned through these 7–Day Shift Sessions, we have all the tools necessary to move forward into each day, grounded in the Truth of the Principle of Divine Love in action.

We are the awareness of that Principle called God. We are God in action.

We can let everything else go, and just be that.

Then we can clearly see the evidence that we are living in and as Grace—now and forever.

Be in the Right Mind, everything else is insanity.

AUTHOR NOTES

T hank you for reading my books! It is for you that I write. If you like what I write, you can help spread the word, and keep my work going, by "liking" my books anywhere the option is offered. I would be honored if you would also post your honest reviews of the book. This will help other readers decide whether it is worth their reading time.

In today's world it is the reader that spreads the word about books they like. If you like mine, anyway you choose to do this will be so helpful. I thank you in advance for all that you do! I hope this book has helped you discover more about the Truth of yourself, and that your life will expand in wonderful ways because of this knowledge.

Now that you have read *The Daily Shift*, why not try more of The Shift Series, or if you like to read fiction too (with happy endings) I have that for you too.

You can find all my books at becalewis.com —Beca.

ALSO BY BECA

The Ruby Sisters Series: Women's Lit, Friendship
A Last Gift, After All This Time, And Then She Remembered, As If It Was Real...

Stories From Doveland: Magical Realism, Friendship
Karass, Pragma, Jatismar, Exousia, Stemma, Paragnosis, In-Between, Missing, Out Of Nowhere

The Return To Erda Series: Fantasy
Shatterskin, Deadsweep, Abbadon, The Experiment

The Chronicles of Thamon: Fantasy
Banished, Betrayed, Discovered, Wren's Story

The Shift Series: Spiritual Self-Help
Living in Grace: The Shift to Spiritual Perception
The Daily Shift: Daily Lessons From Love To Money
The 4 Essential Questions: Choosing Spiritually Healthy Habits
The 28 Day Shift To Wealth: A Daily Prosperity Plan

The Intent Course: Say Yes To What Moves You
Imagination Mastery: A Workbook For Shifting Your Reality
Right Thinking: A Thoughtful System for Healing
Perception Mastery: Seven Steps To Lasting Change
Blooming Your Life: How To Experience Consistent Happiness

Perception Parables: Very short stories
Love's Silent Sweet Secret: A Fable About Love
Golden Chains And Silver Cords: A Fable About Letting Go

Advice:
A Woman's ABC's of Life: Lessons in Love, Life, and Career
from Those Who Learned The Hard Way
The Daily Nudge(s): So When Did You First Notice

Other Places To Find Beca

- Facebook: facebook.com/becalewiscreative

- Instagram: instagram.com/becalewis

- Twitter: twitter.com/becalewis

- LinkedIn: linkedin.com/in/becalewis

- Youtube: www.youtube.com/c/becalewis

ABOUT BECA

Beca writes books she hopes will change people's perceptions of themselves and the world, and open possibilities to things and ideas that are waiting to be seen and experienced.

At sixteen, Beca founded her own dance studio. Later, she received a Master's Degree in Dance in Choreography from UCLA and founded the Harbinger Dance Theatre, a multimedia dance company, while continuing to run her dance school.

After graduating—to better support her three children—Beca switched to the sales field, where she worked as an employee and independent contractor to many industries, excelling in each while perfecting and teaching her Shift System® and writing books.

She joined the financial industry in 1983 and became an Associate Vice President of Investments at a major stock brokerage firm, and was a licensed Certified Financial Planner for over twenty years.

This diversity, along with a variety of life challenges, helped fuel the desire to share what she's learned by writing and speaking, hoping it will make a difference in other people's lives.

Beca grew up in State College, PA, with the dream of becoming a dancer and then a writer. She carried that dream forward as she fulfilled a childhood wish by moving to Southern California in 1968. Beca told her family she would never move back to the cold.

After living there for thirty-one years, she met her husband Delbert Lee Piper, Sr., at a retreat in Virginia, and everything changed. They decided to find a place they could call their own, which sent them off traveling around the United States. They lived and worked in a few different places before returning to live in the cold once again near Del's family in a small town in Northeast Ohio, not too far from State College.

When not working and teaching together, they love to visit and play with their combined family of eight children and five grandchildren, read, study, do yoga or taiji, feed birds, and work in their garden.

Made in the USA
Monee, IL
10 June 2024

59689289R00118